ALWAYS IN STYLE

Doris Pooser

PIATKUS

This edition first published in
Great Britain in 1987 by
Judy Piatkus (Publishers) Ltd of
5 Windmill Street, London W1

British Library Cataloguing in Publication Data
Pooser, Doris
  Always in style
  1. Fashion
  I. Title
  746.9'2   TT507

  ISBN 0 86188 629 1

Phototypeset in 11/12½ Linotron Imprint by
Phoenix Photosetting, Chatham, Kent
Printed and bound in Great Britain by
W. S. Cowell Ltd, Ipswich

CONTENTS

FOREWORD

To be well dressed, a woman must wear clothes that complement her physically, express her personality, are appropriate for the occasion, and are not dated. She must develop her own style. Coco Chanel said years ago that style stays forever and fashion keeps changing. Both style and fashion are important, but we must understand the differences. It is possible to use the very simple guidelines described in this book to develop your own style, and then to reach in the fashion direction you want according to your personality.

I have spent many years researching into colour analysis, originally deciding whether someone had 'warm' Autumn or Spring colouring or 'cool' Winter or Summer colouring. I have worked with dermatologists, skin and hair laboratories, makeup laboratories, colourists and artists, and my research now shows that no one is all warm or all cool. We are a combination of both in varying degrees, but one will predominate. In other words, there will be one seasonal palette that contains the greatest number of complementary colours for you, but all colours in that palette will not be equally successful. These not-so-good colours must be identified and other colours added from a corresponding palette in order to recognise all of your correct colours.

For those of you who may have experienced difficulty in deciding which 'season' you are, in *Always In Style* I explain why this might have been. In the section on colour you will see how to expand your colour palette so that you can begin to wear even more colours. And, as fashion colours change, you'll also learn how to update your wardrobe effectively.

Following the publication of the American and Australian editions of

Always In Style, fashion designers and experts from all over the world have expressed their enthusiasm and agreement with my concepts of style. They agree with me that colour is important, but that it is only the icing on the cake. It is essential first to select clothes that complement your body shape. Would you put the same red dress on the Princess of Wales and the Duchess of York?

Since wearing clothes that complement your body size and shape is the most important part of style, I have started out with a description of body lines. Correctly identifying your body line will help you select clothing that looks like a natural extension of you. Add the correct colours and you will have achieved the first step in identifying your style – wearing clothes that complement you physically. Incorporate your personality, and you can confidently say that you have found your own personal style.

Doris Pooser
October 1986

Introduction

Today, a well-dressed woman creates a picture of herself partly because of her clothes. Colour, design, fabric and details must all balance with her colouring, body size and shape, as well as her facial features. This harmony of design, shape and colour helps express the inner person, also reflected in the way a woman carries herself. These non-verbal messages comprise over half of what she says to others about herself, and they are therefore essential to her style.

But how can we create a balance of clothes and accessories, physical appearance and personality? Most of us have never been taught what to look for when we choose our clothing. We have been heavily influenced by the clothes that look good on our friends, and have therefore never succeeded in defining an individual style, let alone relating it to the clothes we should wear.

Designers have dictated styles of clothing for many years. In the 1930s, Coco Chanel created fashion news in Hollywood because of her suit designs. On and off the movie screen, women were wearing suits. In the 1950s Chanel's new suit confirmed her place in the fashion world. It had a simple straight skirt and the short, collarless jacket had a straight edge-to-edge fastening. The simplicity and versatility of the design became so popular that Chanel's name became synonymous with the style. It became available in all price ranges, colours and fabrics. Looking well dressed was simply a matter of wearing a Chanel-style suit.

Another fashion item for the well-dressed woman was the basic black dress. This had a plain scoop neckline, a straight skirt with fitted waist and long or short sleeves, depending on the season. Socially it was more important to own and to wear a black dress than to be concerned with your appearance in it. After all, a woman was always socially acceptable in her 'basic black'.

Brand names and labels have continued to be important – in casual as well as in formal wear. The emergence of the famous Lacoste alligator illustrates this; a Lacoste shirt has continued to guarantee that good dressing extends to sportswear.

However, in the last twenty years or so, the role of fashion has changed to some extent. In the 1970s, women began entering the workforce in greater numbers than ever before. Because they had few role models, the first generation of working women had to adhere strictly to a dress code in order to achieve credibility and professionalism. 'Dressing for success' meant dressing like men if women wanted to compete in business: navy pin-striped suits, little white blouses and basic makeup became the uniform for the well-dressed businesswoman.

In the 1980s, women have proven their ability in most work areas and have gained credibility and confidence in and out of the workforce. They are ready to express themselves as the creative individuals they are, and are less willing to accept dictation from designers, the fashion industry or arbitrary dress codes.

It is therefore more important than ever for all women to find a style for themselves. Some people can wear an article of clothing and instinctively know that it creates balance and harmony on them. They can select styles that are always right for them and can mix pieces and accessories that create interesting and exciting looks. We often say that these people have a flair for fashion.

In recent years, many books have been written defining categories of style. Most of us have tried to find the look that suits us best, and these books are often helpful.

However, these days we need to wear many different styles, depending on occasion, mood and wish for excitement and change. If we extend the defined categories of style, each of us can consider several.

For instance, a **Dramatic** person is often described as tall and thin, with strong colouring, angular features and a certain sophistication. Does this mean that somebody who is only 5 feet 2 inches tall cannot look Dramatic? Absolutely not! It depends on your definition. Many short women look very good in high-fashion clothing. Some thin, tall and angular women do not look right in high-fashion clothing. Princess Michael of Kent, for example, obviously feels comfortable in conservative clothes and, in spite of her size and shape, she has considered her wishes and personality in the clothing she selects.

If Dramatic is defined as extreme in line and design, very few people are able to dress in a Dramatic style appropriate for all occasions. Some fashion models and entertainers do dress in extreme clothes, are comfortable with their appearance and manage to look right most of the time. Cher is one; she can wear extreme clothing and obviously feels comfortable in it. You need to consider body size, shape and your personality, as well as your likes and dislikes. Therefore, a Dramatic look can be worn by anybody who wishes to do so, once she understands what to look for when selecting individual clothing styles.

A **Classic** type is often described as somebody of medium height with even, well-balanced features, somebody well proportioned with a conservative outlook. But what about the woman who is well balanced, well proportioned and of medium height who is not conservative, or who does not wish to look conservative all the time? She should not be limited or feel stifled by a particular style in which she is not comfortable. Conversely, many women are neither well proportioned nor average in height, but want or need a Classic conservative look.

Classic is, then, a conservative look that most people choose at some time. Some are naturally more conservative than others and will prefer to look 'Classic' more often. However, each of us regardless of size and shape, should have her own Classic look.

Does **Romantic** mean ruffles, glitter and high-heeled shoes? Yes, at times, but we all dress differently for 'romantic' situations, such as having a quiet evening at home with a special person; each of us would wear something different to look romantic in her own style. For example, Jane Fonda, Nancy Reagan and Joan Collins would all dress differently, though each would look romantic. Joan Collins may wear a black satin dressing gown with black lace trim, Jane Fonda a silk smoking jacket with a shawl collar and silk trousers, Nancy Reagan an elegant ivory caftan with a mandarin collar. Each would have her own romantic look, complementing her physically and expressing her individual personality.

A **Natural** is often defined as somebody who is tall, has a sturdy or athletic build, is casual and enjoys informality. However, many people who are born with large bones and who have a sturdy build feel very formal and conservative. Some like to dress up all the time, others enjoy a Dramatic look. Body size and shape should not dictate a style for them, any more than for other people. At times, everybody likes a casual, informal look for a change. Most working women appreciate times when they do not have to get 'dressed up' in the morning, or when they can go without makeup. There are people who are most comfortable with a casual look, and their lifestyles permit this type of dress. However, they must understand the times and places when it is not appropriate and strive for a more professional or business look when necessary.

The chart opposite outlines some appropriate occasions for wearing different 'looks'. Dressing appropriately means looking successful and attractive without feeling uncomfortable. Once this has been understood, your feelings, moods and wishes must be considered. Each of us tends to be most comfortable with one or even two styles; this is fine when we have a choice, but we need different looks at different times. As you build confidence in understanding how your clothes suit you, you will be surprised at your new interest in different types of clothes.

DEFINING YOUR STYLE

None of the descriptions of style tells us what aspects of clothing can be directly related to our physical characteristics. I am not suggesting that labels or classification are wrong; on the contrary, they are interesting, fun and contain a lot of useful information. However, if labels and different styles are used to define your individual style, you must first understand what they mean in terms of your clothing, and how to adapt them to your own body. It is therefore important to learn basic rules that apply to the construction of your clothing, the fabric, design and how they should look on you. By having some guidelines within which to work, you can be sure of wearing exactly what is right for you.

In order to define and determine your own individual style, you must look at your physical characteristics. You were born with a particular body and distinctive facial features. It is time to find the appropriate clothes to complement all your positive characteristics. Once you understand what these are, you will be able to develop your style and flair by combining the right line, designs, fabrics, scale and colours to complement you physically. You can then dress individually and creatively.

Three characteristics of clothing determine its style – line, scale and colour. They can be related to your physical characteristics, for it is important to remember that clothing should balance and harmonise with your body shape, size and facial features. It should look as though it belongs on you, a natural extension of yourself. The silhouette line of your clothing, as well as the detail line, should complement the line of your body and your facial features. The amount of texture and the type of print you wear should be in direct proportion to the line of your clothing. The scale should be in proportion to your body size, and the colours you wear should complement your colouring.

DIFFERENT LOOKS			
	Dramatic	*Classic*	*Natural*	*Romantic*

	Dramatic	*Classic*	*Natural*	*Romantic*
Work	Entertainment industry Fashion industry Department store buyer Boutique owner Art-related industries Interior designer Advertising Magazines, TV and radio Public relations	Business Professional: lawyer, doctor, etc. Worker for political party/fund raising organisation Social worker Teacher Civil servant Estate agent	Teacher Child care worker Work entailing physical labour Work not dealing with public Service-orientated profession	Not appropriate
Casual Leisure Time	Sporting event Picnic Shopping Recreational activity Relaxing	Church function School meeting Civic event Board meeting Political meeting	Sporting event Picnic Recreational activity Shopping Gardening Relaxing	Not appropriate
Social Events	Party, dancing Cocktail party Dinner party Theatre Cinema Wedding Lecture, if group is young	Cocktail party Dinner party Theatre Funeral Lecture Speech Presentation	Resort Holiday area Family-style restaurant	Cocktail party Dinner party Dance Theatre Wedding Formal occasion

Those who are self-employed have flexibility in deciding what is appropriate. The deciding factor should be their audience and/or the people with whom they will be dealing.

PART ONE

LINE

FINDING YOUR BODY LINE

How would you describe your body and facial features? You would probably use a word such as tall, thin, wide, broad, round, curved or straight – all shapes that can be defined in terms of a straight or a curved line. Diamond, triangular, square and rectangular shapes are created with straight lines; oval, round, heart and pear shapes are created with curved lines.

Imagine the shadow of your body projected on a wall by a light shining from behind. You could describe the silhouette outline as straight or curved or as a combination of both. When you look at your body shape from a distance, for example, in a full-length mirror, you may also identify a predominant body shape. (It is best to look at yourself in a leotard and tights so that you see the silhouette of your body and are not distracted by details.)

If you are having difficulty in determining your body line, look at the shape of your face. Often the initial line impression is determined by facial shape and features.

Let us look first at those body shapes with predominantly straight lines. Some women are tall and thin with small flat hips, broad shoulders, small busts and very few curves, others are not especially tall or thin, but have flat hips, square shoulders and square bodies. (Weight is not a factor here; we are looking at the silhouette line, regardless of height or weight.)

Some of these straight lines may appear very sharp, almost extreme, while others are straight but not sharp. On the next few pages are examples of some straight, sharp body lines and some less sharp ones.

Some women have rounded body silhouettes with curved hips, a well

STRAIGHT LINE BODY TYPES

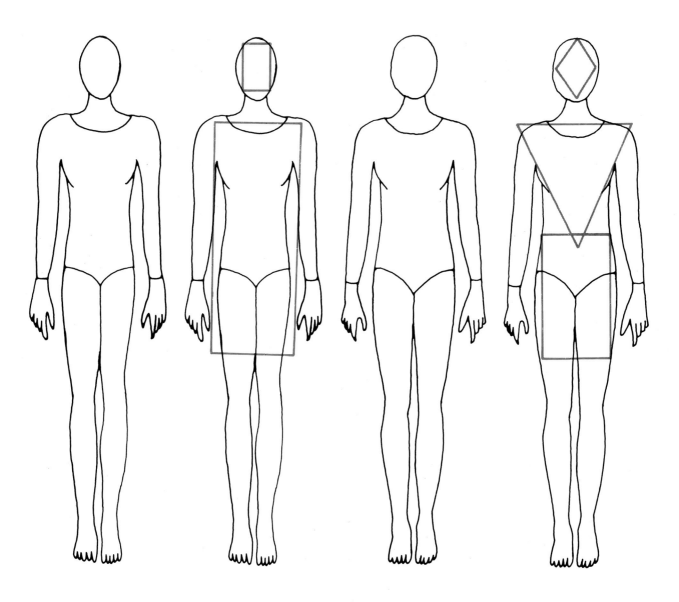

straight   *sharp straight*

CURVED LINE BODY TYPES

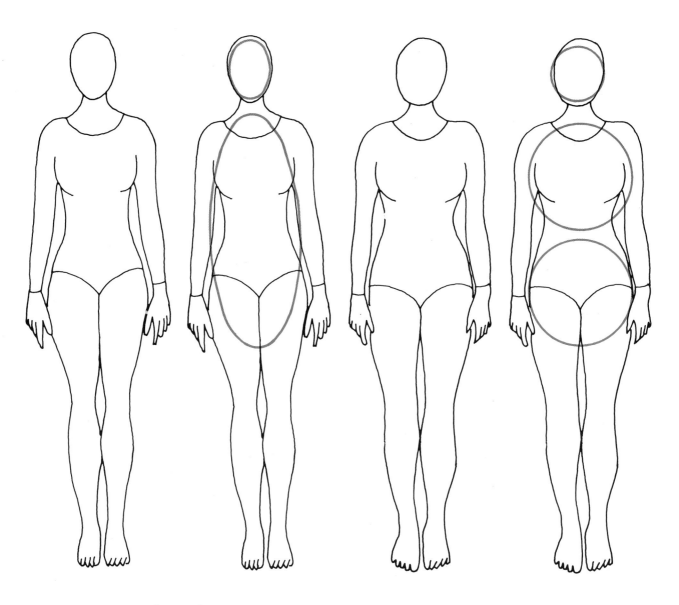

soft curved   *curved*

SOFT STRAIGHT BODY TYPES

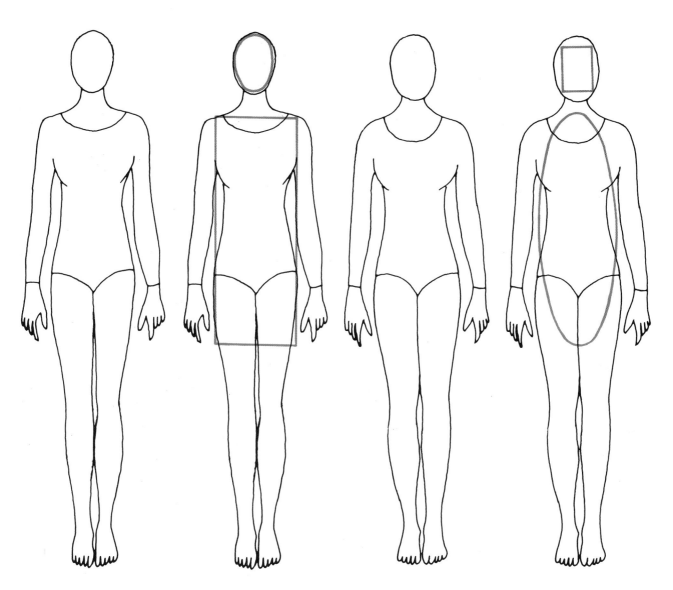

soft straight   *soft straight 2*

defined waist and a full bust. Their facial shape may be oval, round, heart-shaped or pear-shaped. They may have round cheeks, full lips and round or almond-shaped eyes. In any case, a curved line is the predominant body type and it can be round or oval.

If your body is neither very straight nor very curved, it may be a combination of both. A tall woman with curves to her body will often not have a rounded appearance; her height will give the impression that she is straight of line and will make the curves appear less rounded. She will appear to have a softened straight line. Some women who are not tall are neither very curvy nor particularly straight; they too have a soft straight line.

The contrast of a straight facial shape and slightly curved body or the reverse of a curved face and rectangular body will also create a soft-straight line. The combination produces an overall softened straight line.

If you are having difficulty in determining your body line, you probably have soft-straight lines.

Here are two typical questions about body lines.

QUESTION: Whenever I borrow my flatmate's jacket, I look older and feel stuffed into it, even though we wear the same size. Why?
ANSWER: Tailored jackets have straight lines, sharp lapels and square details. You probably need curved lines in your clothing. Look for shawl collars, slightly fitted waists and curved details on your jackets. You can still achieve a classic look that will complement your body by wearing lines that are right for you.

QUESTION: I always admire a flower pinned to a lapel or worn in the hair for evening. But every time I try this look, I feel ridiculous!
ANSWER: You probably have angular features and straight lines to your body. Clothing and accessories with straight lines will look more balanced for you. Try a geometric pin on your lapel or a silk scarf with an abstract design tucked into your pocket.

Look at the drawing opposite showing all these body figures, lined up from the straightest to the most curved. See the gradual movement from one body type to the next? Remember, there are many variations in between, since everyone has a unique and different body shape.

Everyone can be classified along a range from sharp straight to curved, depending on predominant line. Do not try to select an exact point on the line graph or become too concerned about how straight or how curved you are. It is probably sufficient to realise that you are in the straight

BODY LINES

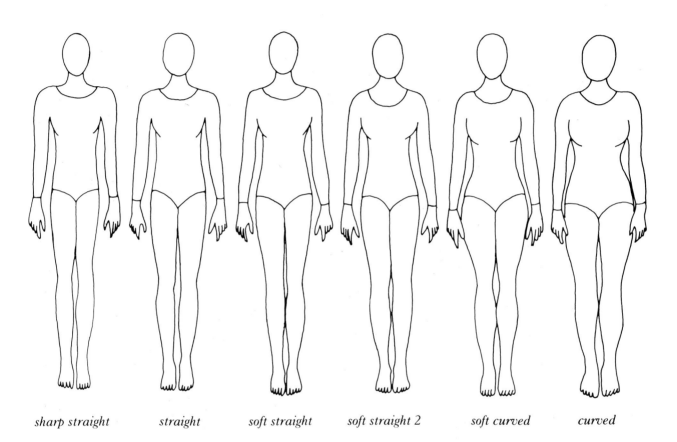

sharp straight   straight   soft straight   soft straight 2   soft curved   curved

range, the curved range, or neither very straight nor very curved, but somewhere between – in the soft-straight range. The charts overlap in the different categories.

Think in terms of a continuum and find a general range where you most clearly fit.

The chart on the next two pages describes facial and body shapes in terms of lines and geometric figures.

FACE AND BODY SHAPES

	Sharp straight	*Straight*	*Soft straight*
Face shape	Diamond Square Triangle	Square Rectangle Oval (with square jaw)	Oval Ellipse
Body shape	Inverted triangle (broad shoulders) Rectangle or some combination with the triangle	Square Rectangle	Rectangle with slight curve
Overall	Triangle (broad shoulders) Angular face, straight body	Rectangle	Ellipse with the slight beginning of a curve
Figure with body shape overlay			

FACE AND BODY SHAPES

	Soft straight 2	*Soft curved*	*Curved*
Face shape	Square Soft edges on square or rectangle	Oval Round	Round Oval
Body shape	Ellipse	Ellipse Oval	Oval or round
Overall	Ellipse, slightly rounded Curved	Oval and defined curve	Round, very curved voluptuous body
Figure with body shape overlay			

The following well known women fit into definite body line categories.

Sharp straight
Cher
Grace Jones
Lorraine Chase
Annie Lennox

Straight
Esther Rantzen
Nancy Reagan
Katherine Hepburn
Queen Elizabeth II
Jacqueline Onassis
Maureen Lipman
Janet Street-Porter
Marti Kane

Soft straight
Jane Fonda
Linda Evans
The Princess of Wales
Felicity Kendall
Margaret Thatcher

Soft curved
Marie Helvin
Paula Yates
Gloria Hunniford
Joan Collins
Anita Ruddick

Curved
Elizabeth Taylor
Dolly Parton
Kiri Te Kanawa
Duchess of York

However, as we leave our teenage years and move through the twenties, thirties and ensuing decades, we rarely retain the same body shape. As we add weight to our frame, our body line tends to soften, as does our facial shape. As a young movie star, Grace Kelly had soft-straight lines in her face and body. As she matured, Princess Grace of Monaco moved across the graph to a soft-curved line. Think back to your teens or twenties and you may notice a comparable progression for your body along the line graph. Although you may notice a movement from sharp-straight to straight, from soft-straight to soft-curved or from soft-curved to curved, you will *not* see a movement from one end of the graph to the other. The bone structure and features you were born with, which are part of you, will always be present. Learn to recognise them and make them the foundation of your personal style.

DRESSING TO SUIT YOUR BODY LINE

There must be a complementary relationship between your clothing and your body line, so that the clothing looks like a natural extension of yourself. Imagine Elizabeth Taylor in a straight skirt and long, straight, double-breasted jacket with sharp lapels. This would not present a balanced image, because she needs clothing with soft contoured lines to balance and complement the curves of her body. A soft wool crêpe suit with a slightly flared or eased skirt, a short jacket with rounded lapels and slightly fitted waist would complement her figure. On the other hand, Jacqueline Onassis would look very good in the straight skirt and jacket because they would complement her straight body and angular face.

Fortunately, today's woman does not need to change or camouflage her body whenever a new 'ideal figure' emerges. She can work with her body line to emphasise its beauty.

By working with your body line when selecting clothing, you will not emphasise problems of too much (or too little) weight, because you will be working with the right line, fabric, print and texture for you. And accept your height. Why wear an unflattering dress so that you can seem a couple of centimetres taller? If you wear the right lines and proportions, nobody will be critical of your height.

Much has been written about how a short person can look taller; for example, by wearing self-fabric belts to create a continuous line in a dress. However, a self-fabric belt on a dress almost always makes the dress look cheap. Always add a leather belt or contrasting tie. If you are short, you can add a contrasting belt – wear it low on your waist or hips – or wear stockings and shoes the same colour as your skirt hem to create a finished look. The positive addition of the belt will far outweigh any negative effect that may result from wearing the wrong belt in order to appear taller. If you are short, accept it. You can enjoy clothes without trying to look taller.

The most harmonious and flattering clothing for your body must have the same line as your body and face shape. Don't try to change your shape: enhance it.

FINDING YOUR CLOTHING LINE

Several lines need to be considered when you look at any item of clothing. One is the silhouette line, the cut or exterior line of the garment. Some clothes have very sharp exterior lines, some very curved ones, with all degrees of straightness and softness in between.

I shall deal with the sharpest, straightest clothing lines and progress to the most curved. Look at the illustrations on pages 28–29.

Straight

The sharp lines of the outfit in the illustration labelled 'sharp-straight' are reflected in its strong angles; in the wide, well-defined shoulders, fastenings and hemlines as compared with the less exaggerated straight lines in the illustration labelled 'straight'.

Soft straight

Continuing across the spectrum, we have what may be called the soft-straight line garment. A soft-straight line is achieved by using exterior construction lines that are smooth and soft with relatively little curve, or by using straight lines with a loose unconstructed fit and/or with a softly woven fabric. The looser construction provides a soft feeling without creating obvious curves. There are two types of soft-straight line garments shown.

Curved

Next is clothing with soft-curved and curved exterior lines. Notice the roundness and softness of the line. Curves are created by the garment's cut and shape, as shown in the following figures.

28   *sharp straight*   *straight*   *soft straight*

soft straight 2   *soft curved*   *curved*   29

Types of clothing can be placed on a line graph in the same manner as different types of body. Thousands of types of silhouette can be placed along the line. The overall impression created by the outline, the flow and the design of the garments determines the predominant external line characteristics. You should be able to identify a general straight line, a curved line or the in-between soft-straight line.

I am *not* suggesting extremes – using circles on round bodies and severe lines on straight bodies. It is only necessary to think in terms of tailored, straight or crisp at one end and a movement to contoured, curved or softened at the other end of the spectrum. Complement the line of your body by using similar lines in your clothing.

CHARACTERISTICS THAT AFFECT CLOTHING LINE

Fabric weight, texture and design affect clothing lines.

Weight

Some of you have fine, delicate facial features and are small-boned, regardless of your weight. You need a fine line in the construction of your clothes to keep them from looking too heavy or bulky for your structure. How do we create a fine line in clothing? By using fine topstitching, stitching close to the edge of the garment, or no topstitching; fine, small buttons, trim and details; fine fabrics such as woop crêpe, fine gabardine, silk, chiffon, bouclés and handkerchief linen.

Some women have bigger bones and larger and stronger facial features. Large bones give you larger wrists, ankles, legs and so on. These are not faults or problems unless you make them stand out or exaggerate them by wearing clothes with too fine a line. The balance would then be lost and you would overpower your clothes. Buy clothes with heavier topstitching, saddle stitching, and stitching that is double-spaced or slightly away from the edge of the garment; heavier and larger buttons, accessories and details and fabric such as wool flannel, medium to heavy gabardine, tweeds, linens, raw silks, satins, knits and similar fabrics. Avoid those that are light or delicate.

Those of you who have neither exceptionally fine features and small bones nor large bones and facial features will have greater flexibility in your fabric selection. Remember, however, that you are looking for *bal-*

ance. Select fabrics that are neither too heavy nor too light for your frame. The traditional silks, cottons, wools and linens come in all weights. The medium weight is best for you. Gabardine, challis, jerseys and satins are all good choices in medium-weight fabrics. Be sure that your details, trim and buttons are neither too small nor too large for a totally balanced look.

The following chart will help you determine whether you have small, medium or large bones and facial features.

YOUR BONE STRUCTURE		
	Wrist	*Ankle*
Small bones	5½ in (14 cm) or less	8 in (20 cm) or less
Medium bones	5½–6 in (14–16.5 cm)	8–9 in (20–23 cm)
Large bones	6 in (16.5 cm) and over	9 in (23 cm) and over

Remember that bone structure must be considered in relation to your overall size. What is small for one person may be average for a shorter person. This chart is for those of average height.

Texture

Texture fabric may be described as rough, nubby or loosely woven. Look at the picture on the next page showing the same jacket with and without texture. Notice that the line is softened by the use of texture at the same time as bulk is added.

Designers often use textured fabrics to create interest in clothing that has muted and monochromatic colours.

It is very difficult to create sharp lines with a loose, nubby or textured fabric. If your clothing needs a sharp line to complement the straight line of your body, you should wear little or no texture. Sharp, straight lines work best with tightly woven fabrics such as wool gabardine or linen, or fabrics with a sheen such as silk, satin or taffeta. The most texture that can be used to effectively create a sharp line is a fine linen, Thai silk or tightly woven twill or tweed. The use of stiff interfacing can also help to achieve a sharp line with a fabric that would otherwise drape or fall softly, as can braid or trim.

Those of you whose bodies are in the curved category will find that texture does not work well. Texture will make your curves look bulky and bumpy instead of smooth and sleek, and you will look overweight (the 'teddy bear' look). Soft, flat fabrics drape well and fall in the soft folds that are so necessary for a curved line. Fabrics such as silks, challis and wool and silk blends are appropriate.

For those who need a soft-straight line, texture is wonderful. It was made to create the exact line you need. Any softly woven fabric with texture automatically falls into soft-straight lines without creating curves. This does not mean that the woman who needs soft-straight lines must wear only textured fabrics. She can wear all types of fabric, including the smooth and shiny ones, as long as she uses the weight that corresponds to her bone size.

If you refer back to the chart on pages 28 and 29, you will see the use of texture with respect to the direction of the line. Those who need the soft-straight line can wear the most texture; less and less is used as you move out to the two extremes of sharp-straight and curved clothing.

Print

Like texture, prints work best when used with the line of the garment rather than against it. Good style dictates that the line of the print should be in tune with the line of the garment, thus creating an elegant and appropriate co-ordination.

FABRIC TYPES AND TEXTURES	
Bouclé	A slightly nubby wool or wool blend knit fabric. The surface finish has small loops or curls.
Broadcloth	A tightly woven smooth fabric, usually of cotton or cotton blends.
Challis	Soft, light-to-medium-weight fabric with a diagonal twill-like weave. It is made in wool, cotton, rayon or a blend.
Chiffon	A sheer, lightweight, flowing fabric, usually in silk or silk blend, which drapes well.
Crêpe	A lightweight fabric of silk, wool or blend with a slightly raised or finely puckered surface. The surface creates a matt finish.
Crêpe de chine	A soft, lightweight crêpe of silk or silk-blend fabric with a slightly raised surface. The surface has a matt finish.
Flannel	A cotton or wool fabric that is medium to heavy in weight with a slightly fuzzy and matt surface. The fuzzy and soft surface makes the fabric moderately soft.
Gabardine	A tightly woven diagonal twill weave that comes in all weights. It is generally a wool or wool blend, but may be found in cotton. Because of the tight weave, it is stiffer than a flannel.
Jersey	A soft fine knit of cotton, wool or blend that has a matt finish and falls softly.
Linen	A fabric with a defined weave because of the sturdy threads. It comes in all weights. It tends to be stiff unless used on the bias or in flared styles.

The sharper and straighter your body line, the more geometric or 'sharp' the print you wear should be. Soft floral prints used in sharply tailored styles do not create a balanced look. Women who need soft, curved lines are better in soft prints and watercolours. A rounded, soft feeling in the print as well as in the construction is essential to total balance. Those who can wear soft-straight lines need designs that are neither too straight nor too curved and that allow for the movement and flexibility of the line. Here, too, they will have some flexibility in their selection of prints, since a geometric print will often be softened just enough by a soft-straight construction.

Notice the categories of prints with respect to line.

Straight

geometric
stripe
abstract
check
houndstooth
Aztec pattern

Soft straight

paisley
stripe
tartan
animal motif
realistic
check
tweed

Curved

floral
watercolour
realistic
rounded
paisley
swirl
scroll

If a line is strong and well defined, the print pattern may vary from it. A small geometric print can often be incorporated into a soft-curved line, a stripe or plaid on the bias will be softened and will often work for a softer line. This combination may not be perfect, but is more acceptable than a floral print made into a tailored style. The soft-

FABRICS, DETAIL AND DESIGN			
	Straight	*Soft Straight*	*Curved*
Small bones	Fine, lightweight, stiff fabric Topstitching at edge Tightly woven fabric Small buttons, details and trim	Lightweight fabric that falls softly – loosely woven Woven Small button, details and trim Topstitching at edge	Lightweight, flat, fine fabrics Fine small buttons and details Fabric that drapes
Medium bones	Average-weight fabric, stiff, crisp and tightly woven Average size detail and trim; topstitching, not edge of jacket	Average-weight fabric woven to fall in soft straight lines Average-sized buttons and trim Topstitching, not at edge	Average-weight fabric that drapes easily Average-sized buttons and detail No topstitching
Large bones	Medium to heavyweight fabric, stiff and tightly woven, large buttons, trim and detail, double or large topstitching	Heavy, loosely woven fabric Large button, trim and detail Double topstitching	Medium-weight fabric Large details and trim No topstitching
Texture	Little to none	Maximum amount	Little or none
Fabric Type	Gabardine, linen, twill, silk, Thai silk, taffeta, satin, moiré, polished cotton, swiss cotton	Linen, Thai silk, challis, tweed, satin, jersey, wool, flannel	Crêpe, challis, raw silk, jersey, chiffon, satin
Print	Geometric, abstract, check, houndstooth, herringbone	Paisley, plaid, check, tweed	Floral, watercolour, rounded, swirl, scroll

straight line may at times combine a floral skirt with a straight jacket to create the overall impression of a softened line.

As a general rule, straight prints may be used in soft-straight or curved construction if, and only if, the construction is well defined. Line and texture should be considered first, then print.

The chart above brings together the major features of fabric type, texture and print for the main body types.

IDENTIFYING DETAIL LINES

Detail lines emphasise and balance the total look of a piece of clothing. Many details can define a specific line. Those that create a straight line should be used on clothing that has straight silhouette lines; details that emphasise curves should be used with curved silhouettes.

For soft-straight silhouettes, it is possible to use straight details as long as the overall impression of the finished piece has a soft flow to it. This can be achieved by using a soft fabric or a single straight line in a garment when the remaining portion of the garment is soft in fit and line. An exaggerated straight line in the skirt can be offset by a cowl neck or shawl collar on the blouse. It is also possible to use some curved details such as a round collar, yoke or pocket, as long as the end result is not totally curved. An unconstructed jacket or straight pleated skirt will balance these curves. Overall, softened straight lines result from softened lines or a combination of straight and curved lines.

The details that best describe each body line type are shown in the chart that follows.

DETAIL LINES			
	Straight lines	*Soft-straight lines*	*Curved lines*
Darts	Long straight darts Sharply defined or no darts	Straight or pleated	Soft gathers instead of darts Soft pleats instead of darts Eased
Seams	Well-defined seam lines Topstitching Contrasting piping, braid or trim	Straight with unconstructed look Self topstitching	Small seams Curved seams No topstitching Fine topstitching Eased
Pleats	Pressed down Stitched down Asymmetrical	Pressed down with soft fabric Unpressed	Soft Unpressed Gathered Eased

Sleeves	Set-in	Set-in	Gathered
	Straight pleat at shoulder	Raglan	Eased
	Square shoulder pads	Dolman	Drop shoulder
	Tapered sleeves	Slightly padded shoulders	Raglan Soft
	Crisp puff	Rounded shoulder pads	Full and billowy
Lapels	Very sharp	Notched with soft fabrics	Rounded
	Notched	Shawl	Curved
	Straight with interfacing	Sloping	Shawl
	Pointed	Rounded	Bias
	Peaked	Sharp or peaked with soft fabric	
Collars	Pointed	Straight with soft fabric	Round
	Notched	Rolled	Rolled
	Straight with interfacing	Cowl	Cowl
	Square	Notched	Notch with round edges
	Stand-up		
	Piped		
Pockets	Well defined	Patch with rounded bottom	Flap
	Square	Slash	Rounded
	Piped	Flap	Set-in
	Slashed	Square with soft fabric	
Jackets	Edge-to-edge fastening	Self-trim	Slightly fitted, well-defined waist
	Square hemline	Subtly defined waist	Rounded bottom
	Fitted or loose	Loose	Curved fastening
	Asymmetrical fastening	Unconstructed	
	Contrasting buttons and trim		
Necklines	Square	Boat	Round
	Boat	Curve	Scoop
	Jewel	Turtle	Draped
	Contrasting trim	Scoop	Flounce
	V	V	Ruffled
	Mandarin	Cowl	Cowl

CLOTHING LINES, DETAIL LINES AND BODY LINES

CLOTHING LINES

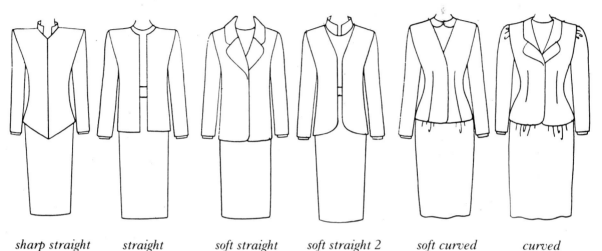

| *sharp straight* | *straight* | *soft straight* | *soft straight 2* | *soft curved* | *curved* |

DETAIL LINES

| *sharp straight* | *straight* | *soft straight* | *soft straight 2* | *soft curved* | *curved* |

BODY LINES

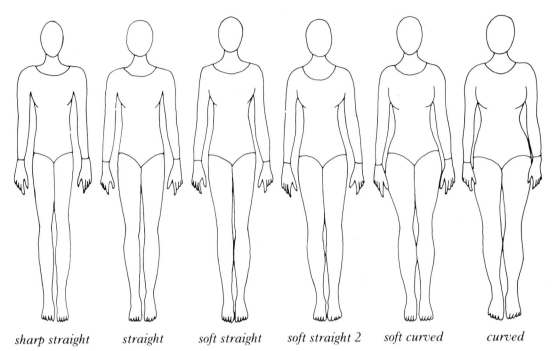

| sharp straight | straight | soft straight | soft straight 2 | soft curved | curved |

On the graph depicting detail lines related to the various clothing lines, notice the movement from one end to the other as the line gradually changes from straight to curved.

Now look at the graph that shows body lines. Notice the direct relationship between the clothing line and the body lines. By looking like a natural extension of these bodies, the clothes create a balance.

International designers

These are the lines the major international designers tend to use most frequently.

Straight lines

Guy Laroche
Chanel
Benny Ong
Yves St. Laurent
Louis Feraud

Castleberry
Jasper Conran
Gucci
Paul Costello

Soft straight

Kenzo

Calvin Klein

Georgio Armani

Bruce Oldfield

Margaret Howard

Missoni

Issey Miyake

Yohji Yamamoto

Escada

Gianni Versace

Jean Muir

Curved

Bellville Sassoon

Zandra Rhodes

Valentino

Emanuel Ungaro

Caroline Charles

Krizia

Emmanuel

Escada

sharp straight   *straight*   *soft straight*   *soft straight 2*   *soft curved*   *curved*

Moderate-priced designers and manufacturers

These are the lines seen frequently in moderate-priced designers' collections. You will be able to find several lines in their collections, which makes it particularly important to begin to recognise the different body lines in clothing construction.

Straight

Stirling Cooper	Mansfield
Stephen Marks	Janice Wainwright
Jeffrey Rogers	

Soft straight

Jaegar	Fenn, Wright & Manson
Windsmoor	French Connection
Alexon	Cache d'Or
Tricotville	Mondi
Gaston Jamet	In-Wear

Curved

Laura Ashley	Monsoon
Norma Kamali	Flora King
Christian Dior	Ralph Lauren
Liberty	

PART TWO
SCALE

Scale
and
Proportion

CLOTHING

N ow you have chosen the best line for your clothing, including the
right print and the correct amount of texture, you should consider
the next characteristic – scale. This can make the difference between
clothing that looks elegant, sophisticated and fashionable and clothing
that looks ordinary.

We have not been made consciously aware of scale. We have all heard
people say, 'I can wear a smaller size if the garment is expensive,' or, 'In
designer clothes, I can buy a size smaller.' The difference is not one of
size; it is one of scale. In fact, when buying the less expensive or non-
designer garment, you should be buying a size larger.

'Scale' can be defined as 'the proportion which the representation of
one object bears to another'. In this case, one object is you, the other is
your clothing, and one should be in proportion to the other. But which
proportion is best? This is easy – it's the proportion at which your
clothing looks not only as if it belongs to you and fits you, but expensive
and elegant. If your clothes are in proportion, you can look thinner if you
are slightly overweight and fatter if you are too thin.

Women whose clothes look elegant and superbly tailored understand
proportion and know that quality is much more important than quantity
when buying clothes. One good, expensive silk blouse is much better
than five cheap ones. For some reason, it is a common misconception that
quantity in clothing is more important: how can anybody wear the same
blouse to the office twice in the same week? However, it is better to wear
the same beautiful blouse every other day than to wear a different one
each day and look and feel ordinary.

When looking for a well-made, good-quality piece of clothing, there are several things to consider.

Seams

Inside seam allowance should be at least ⅝ in (1.5 cm).
Should be finished with zigzag or clean finished.
Line should not pull or wrinkle but should 'hang straight'.
Should be without loose threads.
Exterior stitching should be even and straight, with no loose threads.

Interfacing and facings

Should not wrinkle, gap, or pull.
Should be sewn in rather than fused.
Inside facings should have topstitching or be on bias.

Hemlines

Must hang evenly and straight.
Must be finished with tape or clean finished on the edge.
Stitching must be loose and should not pull.
Stitching should not be visible.

Pockets

Must be straight.
Must be clean finished.
Must lie flat.

Buttons and buttonholes

Should be bone, leather or covered (replace plastic buttons).
Buttonholes should not have loose threads.
Tailor-made buttonholes must be straight.

Belts

Self-fabric belts should be replaced with leather or woven type.
Do not use plastic belts; one neutral leather belt is better than any plastic.

Thread

Colour must match exactly.
Should not be clear plastic.
Should be same type as fabric.

Jackets

Should be fully or half-lined if wool.
Bottom hem should be straight.
Collar and lapel edges should lie flat, not buckle or curl.
Topstitching must be even.

Fabrics

Prints and checks must be matched at all seams.
Fabrics should be natural or blends that look like natural fabric.

Small is not always beautiful

Some women seem obsessed with wearing clothes that do not fit them, and seem to find it necessary to buy the smallest-sized clothes they can possibly squeeze into. There is a common fallacy here: if we can squeeze into a size 10 instead of our usual 12, we must be getting thinner! Psychologically we feel good, though we may not look so wonderful. It is impossible to ignore the fact that too-small clothing looks cheap and skimpy; it can give the appearance of being heavier than you are, because the bulges are visible, or it can make you look too thin, because your bones are showing.

A friend of mine has an attitude that perfectly illustrates this passion for small sizes. She will not consider any garment that is larger than a 10. Whenever I buy a dress or a jacket, hoping to share the joy of my new-found treasure with her, she never says, 'It looks wonderful on you,' or, 'What a lovely colour.' She never even asks how much it has cost. No, her consuming interest is always, 'What size is it?'

It is silly to envy the woman who prides herself on wearing a size 10 or even an 8: it is much better to emulate the woman who wears the proper-sized clothing for her body, regardless of the size given on the tag inside.

Learn to recognise the difference between a dress that is elegant and close-fitting and one that is too tight and looks cheap. Proper fit is a matter of the right proportion, not being too big or too tight. Instead of noticing what size clothing you buy, become aware of how it fits.

The following list will help you determine your proper fit for standard pieces of clothing. It does not deal with length, which we will discuss later.

Blouse

Seam should be on or just outside shoulder bone.

Sleeve should come to wrist bone.

Sleeve should be wide enough to permit at least 1½ in (4 cm) of doubled fabric to be grasped when sleeve is grasped on upper arm.

Buttons must remain closed with at least 1 in (2.5 cm) of fabric on each side of bust line.

At midriff there should be 2 in (5 cm) of doubled fabric as you reach up and grab the fabric from each side; this will allow for proper blousing.

Blouse should be no shorter than hip bone.

Skirt

Pleats should never pull open.

There should be no creases across break of leg.

Pockets must remain closed and should not pull open.

Straight skirts should hang from buttocks in a straight line, not curve under.

Skirt should not ride up when you sit.

There should be at least 1 in (2.5 cm) of extra fabric when you pull the skirt from your body at hip line.

Waistband should be loose enough to allow for two fingers to be inserted.

Thighs must not show.

You should be able to turn your skirt around your body easily.

Knicker line must not show.

Jacket

Shoulder should be at least 1 in (2.5 cm) wider than shoulder bone.

Buttoned, the coat should allow for sweater or blouse and still not pull across shoulder or hip. There should be 1½ in (4 cm) of extra fabric.

Sleeve length should allow for ¼–½ in (0.6–1.25 cm) of blouse sleeve to show.

Sleeve width should allow for blouse or sweater and still have ½ in (1.25 cm) of extra fabric.

Collar must not wrinkle across back.
There should be no pull across back.
Pockets must remain closed.
Any pleat or dart must lie flat.

Trousers

Pleats must remain closed.
Zippers and fastenings must lie flat.
Leg should fall straight from hip with no curve under at buttocks.
Pockets should not gap or pull open.
There must be at least 1–1½ in (2.5–4 cm) of fabric when you pull the
    fabric from your hip bone.
Waist should be big enough to allow the fingers to be inserted.
Knicker line must not show.

What does 'overscaled' mean?

We have now defined scale in terms of fit, so it is time to consider the term
'overscale'. Some of our most famous designers create clothing that is
big, loose and roomy; this is often seen with a label that proclaims 'one
size fits all'. But clothing that is deliberately too big to be loose-fitting on
almost everyone must be considered for balance and proportion, as well
as in terms of a distinctive fashion look.

Who can wear overscale clothing? Most of the designers who create
overscale clothing are designing it for people who are very tall and thin.
Since our ideal is a balance with body size, let us consider a woman who is
5 feet 8 inches tall, and very thin.

She probably has very long arms and legs and looks willowy – even
lanky at times. In a bikini, she may appear 'all arms and legs' and slightly
out of proportion. To make her appear in better proportion, she needs
clothes that are overscaled by normal standards, i.e., out of normal proportion.

A normally scaled outfit such as a Chanel suit or standard jacket will
look skimpy and she will appear to overpower her clothing. She may
appear too thin or too tall.

It is easier for very tall women to wear 'overscaled' clothing. Tall
women such as Jane Fonda, the Princess of Wales and Penelope Keith
need the elegantly loose-fitting overscaled look to balance their height
and their long arms and legs. This overscaling must be in the body and

torso of the garment, as well as in the lengths of sleeves, jackets, skirts and slacks. Longer jackets, longer skirts, fuller blouses and wider shoulders are necessary to balance long arms and legs. Try Long Tall Sally, Eastex, English Lady and Butte Knit, for example.

This is fine if you are tall and willowy, but what if you are average in height, or even short?

Women who are of average height (i.e., about 5 feet 4 inches tall) find it extremely difficult to wear clothing designed for tall people. A woman in this position looks much better in clothing that is proportioned for her scale – in skirt lengths, sleeve lengths and body proportions that are made for her height.

Even though a woman of average height will look lost in an overscaled article of clothing, she is lucky. Almost all the designers whose clothes are sold at moderate prices, as well as the manufacturers in the same category, use an average scale; the woman of average height thus has many more choices.

The woman who is short is likely to have more difficulty in finding properly scaled clothing than her tall or average-sized counterpart. Occasionally, however, designers do produce scaled-down clothing. Many are now designing a special petite scale with shorter arms, shorter skirt lengths, shoulders and midriffs. The total body is scaled down, which is important for a balanced look. Look out for Jaeger's range, and try Marks & Spencer for special lengths.

Your height is the major factor in determining the scale of your clothing. If you are 5 feet 3 inches tall or less, you will have to look for a small or petite scale in your clothing. If you are 5 feet 3 to 5 feet 6 inches you will need an average scale; if you are 5 feet 6 inches or taller, you will need to look for overscaled designs. The person with exceptionally long arms and legs for her height may occasionally be able to wear a scale larger than her height would suggest.

Here is the same garment in three different scales to show you exactly what I mean.

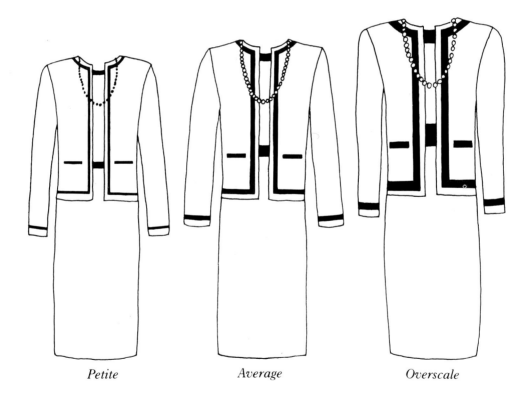

Petite   *Average*   *Overscale*

ACCESSORIES

A friend who has owned and managed several retail stores once commented that the first things she notices about a new customer are her shoes and handbag. She admits that the degree of salesmanship she applies to that customer is strongly influenced not only by the quality of her accessories but by their appropriateness. She understands the importance of scale: Penelope Keith would look unbalanced carrying a small round clutch bag, as would Elizabeth Taylor with an enormous square tote bag.

With accessories, one has a golden opportunity to make an outfit individual and personal. Some people have the ability to add an unexpected accessory that makes what they are wearing stand out in the crowd. They know how to maintain the same line and scale in accessories as they do in their clothing, emphasising angles or complementing curves. A striking belt buckle, earring or necklace will often make the difference between what is ordinary and what is spectacular.

Those who need straight or sharp-straight lines in their clothing should also look for straight lines in accessories. Handbags should be square or rectangular and constructed. An envelope or briefcase looks very good when used with straight lines. A soft, rounded pouch would not be consistent with straight lines of clothing and would therefore detract from the impact of an otherwise striking outfit. With soft-straight lines, an unconstructed soft pouch or an envelope of soft leather creates a balanced look. The soft curved line needs a soft leather bag with small gathers or a bag with a rounded or curved bottom, sides or details.

Do not underestimate the importance of something as apparently insignificant as a belt buckle. Square, rectangular and geometric belt buckles are best with straight lines. A smooth curve, oval or shell complements a soft straight line. Circles, flowers and swirls enhance a curved line.

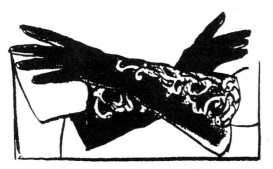

Jewellery

Everyone can wear classic pieces of jewellery such as pearls and chains. Those who need sharp-straight lines may find that seed pearls work better than round ones, or that a clasp with a geometric shape will complement their facial shape better. Pearls in combination with chains or other beads also look less curved. Often pearl earrings can be set in a gold or silver geometric setting to create the right balance of size as well as line. There are many types of chain available. Some have heavy geometric links; others are finer and the links are more curved. It is always possible to combine different pieces of your jewellery to achieve a pleasant and harmonious overall style.

Extremes are never recommended. Contoured shapes are recommended for oval, round, heart and pear-shaped faces. It is often advisable to select an oblong shape for the round face instead of a true circle. Similarly, a round shape will create a balance for someone with an oblong shaped face. Straight, geometric or abstract shapes work well for those with angular face shapes. The square face may do best with rectangular and diamond shapes, using the square carefully. The object is to complement your face and body line, thereby enhancing your features. By choosing shapes related and not necessarily identical to your face shape you will enhance without exaggerating.

HOW TO DISGUISE
COMMON FIGURE FAULTS

Now you know how to work with your body size and shape, not against it, you will find it exciting to express your individuality – to enjoy being you while assured of looking really good.

To help complete your total look, this section on line and scale ends with some final hints on coping with some of your minor flaws.

FIGURE FAULTS			
	Straight lines	*Soft-straight lines*	*Curved lines*
Broad shoulders Shoulders should be 1½–2 in (4–5 cm) broader than hips to allow clothing to hang properly	An asset, emphasising the angle	An asset; you may want to soften them slightly with a V neck, raglan or dolman sleeves	If your shoulders are square, you can soften them with raglan or dolman sleeves Wear curved scoop necklines where possible
Narrow shoulders	If your facial features are extremely angular and your body thin, your shoulders can be extended with large square pads, cap sleeves or epaulettes	Add shoulder pads, boat necks, horizontal detail at shoulders	Add gathers in sleeves, softly rounded shoulder pads, soft draped boat necks
Large hips	Straight dresses with no belt; chemise style Overblouse with straight bottom Eased skirt, as long as it falls straight to maintain a straight line Loosely fitted, dropped belt or dropped waist Stitched-down pleats	Eased, unpressed, gathered or gored skirt Loose overblouse Belts worn low Easement or pleats in waist of trousers and skirts Dresses that fall softly from the shoulders	Eased skirt Flared skirt, soft pleats and gathers Loose flowing top Loose overblouse with slightly fitted waist

	Straight lines	*Soft-straight lines*	*Curved lines*
Large hips (continued)	Straight skirts and trousers that have pleats at the waist and fall straight from the hip. Use tightly woven fabric to maintain straight lines		
Large bust	V neckline Open collars – straight lapels Long sleeves (do not stop sleeve at bust line) No breast pockets or details at bust level Vertical lines Sleeve should not stop at bust line	V neckline Scoop neckline Open collar – straight or curved lapels No breast pockets or vertical detail Sleeve should not stop at bust line	Scoop all necklines Open neck with shawl collar or curved lapels A fuller bust is complementary to this line
Small bust	Adds to the impact of the straight line Horizontal lines can be added Pockets and details at bust line Vertical detail at bust line	Texture, tweed, layering will add volume Loose unconstructed tops so appropriate for this line are perfect Pockets and details at bust line	Bows, drapes, cowl necks and gathers will add curved fullness Yoke, embroidery and soft details at bust line
Long neck	Positive for this look Can add high collar Big jewellery High neckline	Turtle neck High collar Scarves Huge jewellery	Scarves Necklines with bows and gathers, ruffles Jewellery with curved lines Soft, rolled, high collars
Short neck	Open neckline Long necklace V neck	Open necklines Scarves tied low V- or U-shaped neck	U-shaped necks Open collars with bows tied low

MATCHING FACE SHAPES AND HAIRSTYLES

The following are suggestions for enhancing your face shape with an appropriate hairstyle.

Diamond-shaped face

Wonderful cheekbones should be emphasised with angular hairstyles. You may wish to add width across the forehead with fullness or a fringe.

Square face

Emphasise the angles by choosing an asymmetrical style. You may wish to add height to create a balance with total body height by adding fullness on top to lengthen your face.

Rectangular or oblong face

Emphasise angles; try an asymmetrical style. You may wish to shorten the effect with a fringe and hairstyles with no fullness on top to balance the body and neck lengths. An off-centre parting will help.

Round face

Emphasise curves with a soft hairstyle. You may wish to add height to balance the neck and body proportions. Add fullness on the lips.

Pear-shaped face

Emphasise soft curves. You may wish to add fullness across the forehead with soft curls to balance the narrow forehead with the fuller cheeks. Hair brought on to cheeks will soften and diminish cheek width.

Heart-shaped face

Emphasise curves. You may use an off-centre parting to soften the forehead and add fullness at chin level.

HIGH FASHION

OVERSCALE AS A FASHION TERM

What is 'high' fashion? This is an elusive term, but there are a few clues. High fashion can be defined as the styles introduced each year in London, Paris, Milan and New York by the world's leading fashion designers. These cater to those fortunate women who have the desire and the money to own beautifully made status clothing. The colours, fabrics, prints and silhouettes favoured by these designers are immediately copied and reinterpreted for millions of women of more limited means who are just as interested in following current fashion trends.

The second level of fashion has more to do with the real world, where manufacturers create clothing for the great number of women who dress for their day-to-day jobs and lifestyles. These women want to look appropriately dressed and efficient as they pursue their careers. Their clothing styles may lean toward the classic, but they keep their fashion appeal.

There is yet another group of women: the innovators. To these women, fashion means experimenting with the new and often outrageous offerings that spark the volatile fashion scene from season to season. The innovators have the personality and drive that it takes to be first with something new and different. *Which type are you?*

I contend that high fashion is really nothing more than an exaggeration of scale, line, or detail. The recent trend toward overscaled clothing is an exaggeration of scale. (Some of the exaggerated looks, such as the Comme des Garçons which came from Japan several years ago, were so exaggerated that they created a sloppy and unkempt effect. Fortunately, these looks are being replaced by a more attractive exaggerated proportion.)

How much exaggeration is appropriate? In order to avoid an extreme or trendy image and still achieve an exaggerated fashion look, it is important to exaggerate the scale by one size beyond your elegantly loose fit. It is important to watch the trends from season to season as designers enjoy the challenge of change.

Who can wear the exaggerated or high-fashion looks? It all depends on who you are inside. If you have the desire, personality, and knowledge to wear the look – and wear it with confidence – you can do it. You now have the knowledge to find your right line and scale. Let's find out if you have the personality to exaggerate it!

* At the end of the book I will tell you how to send for your *Always in Style Portfolio*. Each season you will receive a new edition to enable you to keep abreast of the trends. The portfolio will interpret these trends for your particular body line, so that there will be no more guessing about which of the new styles will be the most complementary for you.

ARE YOU READY FOR A HIGH-FASHION LOOK?

Here are some simple questions relating to your personality. Please answer them honestly.

Are you outgoing and extroverted?
□Yes   □No

Are you the first in your group to try a new hairstyle?
□Yes   □No

Do you love the unexpected?
□Yes   □No

Do you enjoy being noticed?
□Yes   □No

Are you sophisticated?
□Yes   □No

Do you love clothes?
□Yes   □No

Are you conservative and cautious?
□Yes   □No

Have you had the same or a similar hairstyle for several years?
□Yes   □No

Are you satisfied with your current wardrobe?
□Yes   □No

Are you applying your makeup in the same way you did five years ago?
□Yes   □No

Do you keep your skirt length the same year after year?
□Yes   □No

Are you shy or reserved?
□Yes   □No

If you answered 'Yes' to the first six questions, you are ready for a high-fashion look. If you answered 'Yes' to the last six, you are more conservative, but still want to strive for a fashionable look. If your answers were mixed, you probably don't wish to dress in the height of fashion, though you still wish to be stylish.

Remember that conservative and high fashion are *not* two separate looks. Instead, there is a whole spectrum from the most extreme to the most conservative, with many steps along the way. You can, therefore, experiment with current fashion. Lengthen or shorten a skirt a little more than average, add a looser top and new belt, wear flat shoes or loose trousers. If such things work for you and you feel comfortable, keep going. Some of you will reach further than others.

Those of you who have no desire for a high-fashion look may be comfortable with an elegantly loose fit and your proper line. That is fine; you can look current and fashionable, even though you are conservative. Lengthen or shorten your skirt just a little, add a new jacket, add small shoulder pads to your dress or jacket. Update your look. Those of you who want the high-fashion look will have to exaggerate more. Add larger shoulder pads, wear skirts to your ankle or above your knee. But be sure to start with your proper fit and scale it up slowly, until you reach a maximum of one size larger than your elegantly loose fit.

As always, there are certain guidelines to consider in determining just how long or short you can wear your jackets and skirts for either a fashionably conservative or a high-fashion look and still adapt the lengths to you personally. I have already suggested scaling up your clothing by one size. Now, let's look at your possible lengths.

MAINTAINING PROPORTIONS

'Ideal' body proportions

The ideal body is supposed to be in four equal portions, from the top of the head to the underarm; from the underarm to the break of the leg; from the break of the leg to the knee; and from the knee to the floor.

If your body is not equally proportioned according to this scale, this is not a problem: many people are longer or shorter in some areas of their bodies than in others. However, it is important to understand *where* you are long or short, so you can alter skirt or jacket lengths as fashion trends change. You can therefore adapt any fashion for yourself.

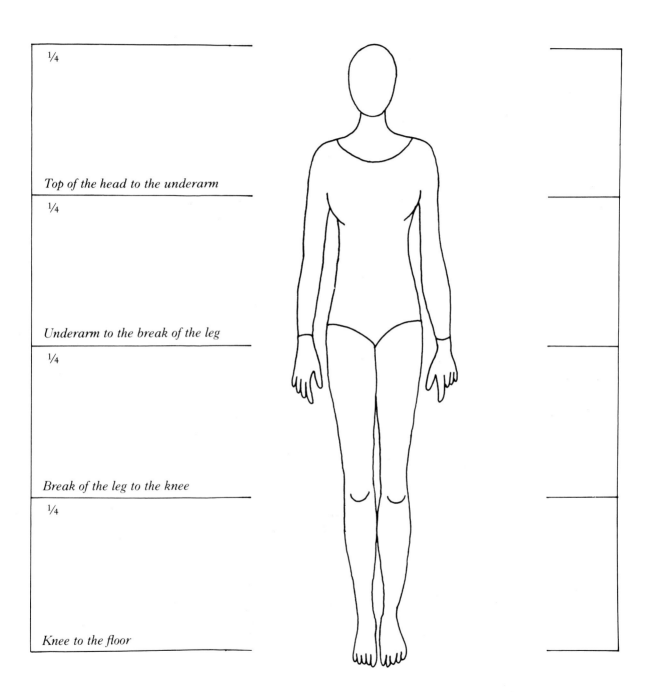

¼

Top of the head to the underarm

¼

Underarm to the break of the leg

¼

Break of the leg to the knee

¼

Knee to the floor

For instance, you can change the length of your legs visually by changing your jacket length – but the extent to which you can change it depends on your individual proportions.

The first thing you must do is to decide what look you are trying to achieve. Most of us wish to look fashionable and are inclined towards the most currently acceptable look. But some say they would like to find one length for their skirts and jackets and stick to it forever! This is certainly more convenient than feeling compelled to alter your look every now and again, but it can also make you look outdated. If you have the same clothing you wore years ago, you may also look older.

The effect is the same if you put on your makeup in exactly the same way, with the same colours, the same amount of eyeliner or shadow and the same quantity of pancake makeup or foundation that you used when you were a teenager and just learning to apply makeup.

Certainly, it is a little more trouble to alter your hems from time to time, to add shoulder pads or subtract them, or add or subtract features such as lace trim or fringing, but if you attempt to dress according to the current fashion to at least some extent, you will look younger; as though you care enough about yourself to spend extra time and effort on your appearance. Very little is usually necessary to update clothing – perhaps nothing more than an inch or a couple of centimetres in one direction or the other.

Your own proportions

Determine which quarters of your body are longer and which shorter than the others. If you are long or short in proportion from your head to your underarm, this is not particularly important; leg and torso length are more so.

If your leg is long from knee to floor, you can wear your skirts very long when the styles are long and still have enough leg showing for the skirt to be flattering. If short skirts are in style, you must be careful; if you wear your skirt too short, your leg will look so long that it will seem out of proportion. You can achieve the look of a shorter skirt by wearing your skirt a little longer and lengthening your jacket. The result: your skirt will appear shorter. You have managed to achieve a fashionable look and still complement your leg.

If your leg is short from the knee down and you want to wear long skirts, you must be careful. In order to have enough of your leg showing for the skirt to be flattering, you cannot make your skirt too long. You don't have enough room. However, you can shorten your jacket, which

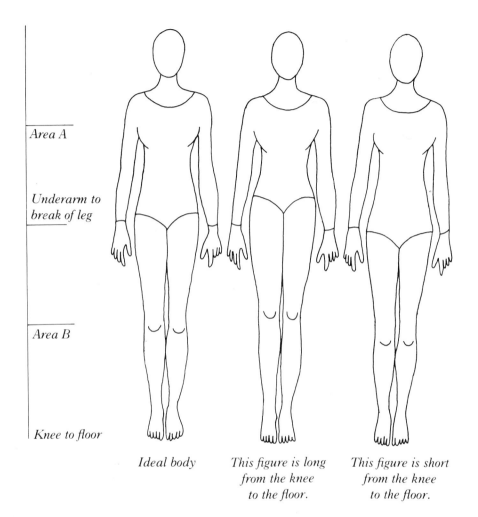

Area A

*Underarm to
break of leg*

Area B

Knee to floor

Ideal body

*This figure is long
from the knee
to the floor.*

*This figure is short
from the knee
to the floor.*

will make the skirt appear longer. You will able to wear very short skirts when they are in style, but you must be careful that your jacket is not too long.

In the days when the Chanel suit was in style, the fashionable look was one of equal proportions. This, too, can be achieved by changing your skirt and jacket lengths. Use this information to create the look you want, rather than as a means of 'judging' the perfection of your body. Your body and facial size and shape and your proportions are *you*. Work with them to develop your own style.

These charts summarise your total style. Select your right body line and fill in the blanks where necessary.

YOUR SHAPE AND LINE

	Straight lines	*Soft-straight lines*	*Curved lines*
Body shape	Triangle Rectangle Square	Rectangle Ellipse	Oval Circle
Face shape	Diamond Rectangle Square	Oval Square Oblong Rectangle/softened	Oval Heart Pear Round Rectangular

Clothing line	Straight exterior line
	Straight detail line
		Soft-straight exterior lines
		Straight exterior lines
		  with soft fabric and
		  unconstructed lines
		Straight details on soft fabric
		Contoured exterior lines
			Curved exterior lines
			Curved details
			Soft-straight details

YOUR FABRIC (Choose one detail in your line)

	Straight lines	*Soft-straight lines*	*Curved lines*
Fine fabric/small details	☐	☐	☐
Average weight fabric/average details	☐	☐	☐
Heavyweight fabrics/large details	☐	☐	☐

YOUR TEXTURE

	Straight lines	*Soft-straight lines*	*Curved lines*
Your texture	Little	Maximum	Little
Print	Geometric Abstract Stripe Plaid Herringbone Houndstooth Check	Stripe Paisley Plaid Tweed	Floral Watercolour Swirl Rounded

YOUR SCALE			
	Straight lines	*Soft-straight lines*	*Curved lines*
Overscale	☐	☐	☐
Average scale	☐	☐	☐
Petite	☐	☐	☐
Accessories	Geometric/angular Constructed Square Diamond Rectangle	Geometric/soft Unconstructed Constructed with soft 　material Oval Ellipse	Curved Soft constructed Round Floral Oval

YOUR ACCESSORIES			
	Straight lines	*Soft-straight lines*	*Curved lines*
Large (overscale)	☐	☐	☐
Medium (average)	☐	☐	☐
Small/medium (petite)	☐	☐	☐

YOUR FASHION DIRECTION			
	Straight lines	*Soft-straight lines*	*Curved lines*
High fashion (exaggerated scale and accessories)	☐	☐	☐
Conservative high fashion (slight exaggeration)	☐	☐	☐
Conservative fashionable (classic with fashion direction)	☐	☐	☐

PART THREE
COLOUR

THE FINAL DIMENSION

Films have fascinated the public from their earliest beginnings in grainy black and white. But their success skyrocketed with the introduction of colour. Why was this so? Films and television literally 'came alive' with colour, because colour has both a dimensional and an emotional effect on each of us. The performers, who had been little more than remote images on screen in black and white, became real people in colour.

Colours have a profound effect on us. They evoke emotions, pleasant or unpleasant. Colour tests are often used to investigate the problems of people who are unwilling or unable to communicate on a verbal level.

Dressing in the style that is right for you is generally more important than dressing in the right colour, but the combination of both has a greater effect on your appearance than each separately. This is a case in which the whole is more than the sum of its parts.

By analysing your body type, we have determined what style of clothing suits you best. Going beyond the visual analysis, we have incorporated your personality traits to add another dimension to your wardrobe. That final dimension is colour. Now we need to analyse your colouring in order to determine the best colours for you to wear. We will then be able to consider your personality, to add the final dimension to your style.

THE SEASONAL COLOUR SYSTEM

The seasonal colour system uses the four seasons – Summer, Autumn, Winter, Spring – to describe your colouring and the range of colours (or palettes) that flatter you.

Every woman can describe her colouring by a seasonal palette. The Winter woman looks most striking in cool colours with sharp contrast; the Summer's colouring is best complemented by the cool, dusty colours of summertime, the Autumn woman looks best in rich, warm colours and muted earth tones; Spring's colours are warm and fresh.

In the seasonal palettes, colours are grouped by undertone, depth and clarity of colour. Winter colours are blue-based, deep and bright, and Summer colours are blue-based, lighter and muted. The Autumn colours are gold-based, deep and muted, and the Spring colours are gold-based, lighter and bright. In each case three characteristics have been described – undertone, depth and clarity.

By considering the same three characteristics (undertone, depth and clarity) of skin tone, hair and eye colour as we did for colour palettes, it is possible to find the seasonal palette that best describes each person's colouring. In the past, men and women have been described as 'seasons' by a seasonal palette – one and only one palette. After four years of research, and after testing thousands of people as well as working with dermatologists and cosmetic labs, I have found that we can in fact find a seasonal palette that contains the greatest number of your best colours. However, there are some colours in that palette that are not your best. There are also colours from related palettes that will be excellent on you. It is therefore necessary to add colours from a secondary palette to complete your own individual palette.

The first step is to find the palette that contains the greatest number of complementary colours. You can then complete your palette by expanding the seasonal colour system. Let us consider basic characteristics, season by season. I have incorporated the latest findings in the individual descriptions. These will confirm the need to expand the four palettes and the logic behind it.

WINTER

Skin

Winter women have a predominant blue undertone to their skin, though this is often subtle and difficult to see. Many Winters have grey-beige skin, ranging from light to dark, usually with no visible pink. Many olive-skinned people are Winters. Winters may have some evidence of 'warm' in their skin tone such as freckles or a true beige colour. The 'warm' will not, however, be a dominant characteristic.

Many Winters are sallow, appearing yellow, and wrongly believe they belong to another seasonal group. Do not confuse sallowness with a golden skin tone. Wearing golden colours increases the sallowness of their complexion, while the cool Winter colours make the sallowness disappear. A Winter may also have extremely white skin and dark hair. The white may have a visible pink tone, but more often it does not. Winters usually do not have rosy cheeks.

Hair

Winters usually have medium to dark brown or black hair, often glossy. The Winter woman tends to go grey dramatically, either reaching a salt-and-pepper stage or turning steely white. Winter hair usually has an ash tone, though sometimes the hair will have red highlights that are visible in sunlight (this is not the metallic red that is seen in Autumn hair). However, it does indicate some warm undertone. Everyone's hair at some level has red in it. The red is, in fact, a warm red. On the Winter person this will be subtle.

Eyes

Winter eyes can be black-brown, red-brown, green, blue or hazel; they are most often a deep colour. Regardless of colour, the eye will have a grey or ash tone to the iris. The hazel or brown eye will at times look warm.

In general, Winter eyes tend to have a look of high contrast between the whites of the eyes and the iris. This clue is especially helpful if you are deciding between Winter and Summer, as the white of a Summer eye is usually much softer, with less contrast in the iris.

Note: Most recent studies indicate that Winters may have some evidence of 'warm', either in their hair colour, eye or skin tone. However, this warm element will not be strongly obvious. The overall impression of the total will be cool, deep or bright. It is very important to understand which characteristic best describes your Winter colouring.

Tick the characteristics that describe you.

Skin

- ☐ Very white
- ☐ White with slight pink tone
- ☐ Beige (no cheek colour, may be sallow)
- ☐ Grey-beige or brown
- ☐ Rosy beige
- ☐ Olive
- ☐ Black (blue undertone)
- ☐ Black (sallow)

Hair

- ☐ Blue-black
- ☐ Dark brown (may have red highlights)
- ☐ Medium ash brown
- ☐ Medium brown
- ☐ Salt and pepper
- ☐ Silver grey
- ☐ White
- ☐ Chestnut brown

Eyes

- ☐ Dark red-brown

☐ Black-brown
☐ Hazel (brown plus blue or green)
☐ Grey-blue
☐ Blue with white flecks in iris (may have grey rim)
☐ Dark blue, violet
☐ Grey-green
☐ Green with white flecks in iris (may have grey rim)

Typical Winter Colours

Winter colours are dark, vivid, and blue-based. Avoid all colours with strong golden undertones such as orange, peach, gold, yellow-green, orange-red and tans. There are some true colours in the Winter palette that have equal warm and cool undertones that will be excellent on some Winters. If you must wear brown, choose a dark brown that is dark enough to wear with black shoes and belt. Avoid pastels and all dusty, muted colours. Lighter colours are added to Winter's palette to create a contrast look when used with their deeper colours. Dark-skinned Winters may find that taupe and the light and medium greys are best when worn with other, brighter colours near the face. It is necessary to understand which of the Winter colours are your best.

White

Winter is the only season who can wear pure white. You are never boring in a white blouse or T-shirt! You may also wear the soft white that suits Summer so well (but not ivory or yellowish white), though the bright white will look more striking on you.

Black

Winters can wear black most successfully. This is because you can take a high-contrast look more readily than any other season. There are some Winters who are better in charcoal since black becomes heavy on them.

Grey

Your greys range from charcoal to icy grey. The best will be true grey, not yellowish or blue. Many Winters, especially those whose hair has turned grey, may add blue-greys to their palettes.

Taupe (Grey Beige)

Your beige is not tan-toned, but a taupe colour. When you wear it next to your face, it must be light and clear. You may choose a darker shade in accessories. In general, beige is a difficult colour for a Winter to wear unless used with another contrast colour.

Blue

Navy blue is excellent on you. You may wear any shade of navy near the face. Your other blues are true, royal, Chinese and turquoise, all deep or bright. Most Winters can also wear periwinkle blue.

Red

Winter's reds are either true or blue-reds, including burgundy. Your burgundy must be clear, sharp and bright. Some Winters can also wear muted or brownish tone burgundy. Many Winters are better in their true reds and must be careful that the burgundy does not get too dark.

Green

Your greens range from a true green to emerald to pine. Pine is similar to Autumn's forest green, except that it has a blue cast rather than a yellow one. You can see this difference by comparing the two colours side by side.

Yellow

You can wear only a clear lemon yellow, not gold. Some Winters can wear the bright gold of Autumn, especially when mixed with black, charcoal or navy.

Pink and Purple

Winter's pinks and purples are deep colours. Shocking and deep hot pinks are less conservative; magenta and fuchsia are quite sophisticated colours, but are too strong for some Winters.

SUMMER

Skin

Summers often have visible pink in their skin, so it is easy to see the blue undertone. Some Summers are very fair and pale, with little pink rings under the skin on the whitest parts of their bodies. Other Summers have a rose beige skin or sallow beige skin, making the blue undertone difficult to see. A sallow Summer makes an especially dramatic improvement in her appearance when she wears her cool colours. Some Summers may have evidence of a warm undertone. This may be visible in a light beige skin tone or freckles on the face. The rosy appearance will dominate. In addition, a cool, powdery look will be apparent.

Hair

As a child, Summer is often blonde, her hair colour ranging from white to golden to ash blonde. During adolescence, her hair tends to darken, and may become a light ash brown. Summer blondes bleach quickly in the sun, so often a Summer woman has brown hair in the winter and blonde hair in Summer. Brunette Summers have hair with an ash tone, ranging from very light to dark brown. The Summer woman's hair greys gradually to soft salt and pepper, blue-grey or pearly white. Grey is a cool colour that blends well with the ash tones of her hair, giving her a distinguished look.

Eyes

Summer eyes are usually blue, green, grey or hazel, with a cloudy look to the iris. Hazel eyes have a soft, grey-brown smudge around the pupil with edges blending into blue or green. The iris in a blue or green eye has a white webbing throughout, giving the appearance of cracked glass. Some Summers have soft rose brown or grey-brown eyes. This is most common in black or Asian races. It is rare to see a brown eye on a Summer. The whites of a Summer's eyes are creamy, in soft contrast to the iris, as opposed to a Winter, whose eyes have sharp contrast.

Note: Recent studies have shown that even Summers may have some warm elements to their colouring. The cool, rosy and soft look will predominate. Occasionally some warm freckles can be seen. There are very few true Summers. The overall impression will be cool, light or muted. It is important to understand which characteristic best describes your Summer colouring.

Tick the characteristics that describe you.

Skin

☐ Pale beige with pink cheeks
☐ Beige with no cheek colour (even sallow)
☐ Rosy beige
☐ Very pink
☐ Grey-brown
☐ Rosy brown

Hair

☐ White blonde
☐ Ash blonde
☐ Golden blonde
☐ Warm ash blonde (slightly golden)
☐ Dark ash blonde
☐ Ash brown
☐ Dark brown (taupe tone)
☐ Brown with auburn cast
☐ Blue-grey
☐ Pearl white

Eyes

☐ Blue (with white webbing in iris, cloudy look)
☐ Green (with white webbing in iris, cloudy look)
☐ Soft grey-blue
☐ Soft grey-green
☐ Bright clear blue
☐ Pale, clear aqua (eyes change from blue to green, depending on clothes)
☐ Hazel (cloudy brown smudge with blue or green)
☐ Pale grey
☐ Soft rose brown
☐ Grey-brown

Typical Summer Colours

The Summer colours are light, muted and blue-based. The Summer image is enhanced by soft contrasts and colour combinations. Fair Summers with blonde or light hair should use the darkest colours, such as burgundy, deep blue-green and dark blue-red, with care; large areas of these dark colours may be too strong next to the face.

Soft White

The most flattering white for you is soft but not yellow. It has less 'blue' than Winter's pure white.

Rose Beige and Brown

Your beige must always have a rose tone, rather than an ivory or yellow one. You can wear browns from medium to dark as long as they, too, are rose toned. Your browns are especially flattering if they are muted (greyish).

Blue-Grey

Summer may wear all blue-greys from light to dark, but should be careful with true greys or yellowish greys. Greys without any blue may look good on some Summers.

Blue

Your navy is greyish, more flattering to you than a bright or black navy. You may wear almost all other blues, light medium or dark, but not the extremely bright or royal blues of Winter. Your blues may be clear or muted, and your lighter blue clothes will have a lot of grey in them. You can also wear periwinkle, a blue with violet in it.

Green

Your greens are all blue-greens, ranging from a light pastel to medium blue-green and to a dark blue-green. The greens are very good on brown or hazel-eyed Summers.

Yellow

Summer's yellow is a light lemon; avoid yellows that are golden. Some Summers can wear a buff or banana yellow very well.

Pink

Your pinks are blue-toned, ranging from light and medium shades to deeper rose and fuchsia colours. Although you may wear bright pinks, be careful not to buy the intensely clear and bright shades from the Winter chart. Warm pinks will often look good on light-haired Summers.

Red

Summer's reds range from raspberry and watermelon to blue-reds. Some Summers may wear dark blue-red as well as burgundy and all wine colours, though they are often too dark.

Plum

Plum is your version of purple. It is a greyish purple, not as intense or as dark as the royal purple of Winter. It is often too deep for all Summers except those with dark hair. Lavender, orchid and mauve are very good colours for you.

Avoid pure white, yellowish beiges, deep tans and browns, gold, orange, peach, orange-reds and yellow-greens.

AUTUMN

Skin

Autumns have golden undertones to their skin. There are three basic Autumn shades and colour combinations: the fair-skinned woman with ivory or creamy peach skin; the true redhead, often with freckles; and the golden beige woman whose skin ranges from medium to deep copper. Autumn's skin will often have an absence of colour to it, projecting a very muted look. Many Autumns are pale and look better in their darker or richer colours.

Hair

Autumn's hair contains obvious red or golden highlights. It ranges from auburn to copper, strawberry blonde to red, dark golden blonde to warm brown. Some blonde Autumns have hair often referred to as 'ash blonde' and these can easily be confused with Summers. A few Autumns have charcoal hair. Autumn hair, except for that of a few auburns and dark brunettes, may have a matt rather than a shiny finish. The Autumn woman does not usually go grey dramatically because the grey is warm and soft. Once her hair has turned completely grey, it looks harmonious and has a warm, golden cast.

Eyes

Autumn eyes are usually golden brown or green with orange or golden streaks radiating from a star formation that surrounds the pupil. Sometimes there are isolated brown specks in the iris. Some Autumns have clear green eyes, like glass, or deep olive green cat eyes. There are few vivid blue (turquoise) and teal blue Autumn eyes that are marked by a teal grey rim around the edge of the iris.

Note: Recent studies indicate that Autumns may have some cool elements in their colouring. This can be observed in some ash in the hair, a rosy look or ruddiness to the complexion, or some grey or blue in the eye colour. The total effect will still be warm, deep or muted. It is important to understand which characteristic best describes your Autumn colouring.

Tick the characteristics that describe you.

Skin

☐ Ivory
☐ Ivory with freckles (usually redhead)
☐ Peach
☐ Peach with freckles (usually golden blonde, brown)
☐ Golden beige
☐ Beige
☐ Dark beige (coppery)
☐ Golden brown

Hair

- ☐ Red
- ☐ Coppery brown
- ☐ Auburn
- ☐ Golden brown (dark honey)
- ☐ Golden blonde (honey)
- ☐ 'Ash' blonde
- ☐ Strawberry blonde
- ☐ Charcoal brown or black
- ☐ Golden grey
- ☐ Oyster white

Eyes

- ☐ Dark brown
- ☐ Golden brown
- ☐ Amber
- ☐ Hazel (golden brown, green, gold)
- ☐ Green (with brown or gold flecks)
- ☐ Clear green
- ☐ Steel blue
- ☐ Teal blue
- ☐ Bright turquoise

Typical Autumn Colours

Autumn colours are generally muted, but they always have warm, golden undertones. A clear colour looks pure and clean; a muted colour is toned down by adding brown, grey or gold. There are a few clear colours in the Autumn palette, but most Autumns prefer their medium or bright colours slightly muted. The Autumn palette gains its power from an artful combination of blended tones with the more assertive, dark colours.

Oyster White

Your best white is oyster (beigy white). You may also wear ivory and the soft white from the Summer palette, but never pure white, which will make you look pale.

Brown and Beige

All your beiges and browns are warm, earth tones. Your dark chocolate brown and mahogany are rich colours, too dark for some Autumns. Camels, khakis and tans are good for all Autumns. Your bronze is an unusual colour, flattering only to some Autumns.

Blue

A marine navy is the only navy that truly flatters the Autumn, but it is hard to find. You can wear any kind of teal blue, though the darker and richer the colour the better. Your turquoise is medium to dark and has warm, yellow undertones. By comparing turquoises in the shop, you can see that some are clear and bright (not for you), while others are yellower and slightly muted. In general, you look best in a deep periwinkle blue, a colour with a violet cast. A deep purple also looks good on many Autumns.

Green

Your greens range from dark forest green to olive, jade and greyish greens. You can wear any green that has a golden tone, from subtle to bright. The light grey-greens are best on those Autumns with 'Summer-like' colouring. The darker greens are good on Autumns with dark hair and eyes and should be used with care by lighter or more golden Autumns.

Gold and Yellow

Your golden colours are plentiful. Choose gold in a quality fabric, or the garment you are wearing will look cheap. You can wear any shade of gold, from mustard to a bright yellow-gold. Some Autumns must be careful and wear their golds as accent colours.

Orange

Your oranges include terracotta and rust colours, which are easy to find in all types of clothing. Your pumpkin and bright orange are accent colours, good in prints or in solids for the less conservative.

Peach and Salmon

Your best peach, apricot and salmon shades are deep. Use the light version mixed with darker or brighter colours to add emphasis. Salmon is your version of pink.

Red

You may wear any red with an orange base, ranging from bright orange-red to bittersweet red and dark tomato (more muted shades). Your reds may become brownish, resembling maroon. Avoid burgundy, as it is too 'blue' and harsh for you and may bring out any lines in your face.

SPRING

Skin

Look for the golden undertone. The Spring woman's skin is ivory, peach, pink or golden beige, and she often has rosy cheeks or blushes easily. Some Springs are ruddy and can easily be confused with Summers because of their apparent pinkness. This is due to their delicate or translucent skin. Even their knuckles may look purple. Freckles, usually a golden tan colour, come naturally to the Spring woman. Other Springs have a clear, creamy skin. Even if she has freckles, the Spring woman's skin usually has a clear, bright quality. Black and Asian Springs have light golden or ivory skin.

Hair

Spring's hair is flaxen blonde, yellow blonde, honey, strawberry, golden or dark brown. Springs may have ash-toned hair. Grey is usually yellowy or creamy toned on a Spring. There is an occasional black-haired Spring. If her hair is light, the grey often blends beautifully, making her look 'blonde'. On a dark-haired Spring, the grey may appear white and silvery like Winter's grey. The light-haired Spring woman may wish to cover her grey hair until she has gone completely grey. Once the two-toned look is gone, her grey hair is beautiful, with a pale, warm, dove grey tone. Spring women often go from grey to a cream white, a softly elegant look.

Eyes

Spring's eyes are most often blue, green, teal or aqua, often with golden flecks in the iris. Some Spring women have eyes as clear as glass, giving the impression of a clear ring surrounding the pupil. Some Springs have brown eyes, but they are always golden or topaz. A Spring's hazel eyes contain golden brown, green and gold. A few Spring women have eyes of deep blue that appear to be steel grey from a distance.

Note: Most recent studies indicate that Springs may have some 'cool' qualities. This is often seen in the dark-haired Spring whose hair can range from ash brown to black. The deep, clear blue eyes of some Springs also occasionally appear cool. Overall, the impressions will be warm, golden or bright. It is important to understand which of these characteristics best describes your Spring colouring.

Tick the characteristics that describe you.

Skin

☐ Creamy ivory
☐ Ivory with golden freckles
☐ Peach
☐ Peach/pink (may have pink/purple knuckles)
☐ Golden beige
☐ Golden brown
☐ Beige
☐ Rosy cheeks (may blush easily)

Hair

☐ Flaxen blonde
☐ Yellow blonde
☐ Honey blonde
☐ Strawberry blonde (usually with freckles)
☐ Strawberry redhead (usually with freckles)
☐ Auburn
☐ Golden brown
☐ Ash brown
☐ Red-black (rare)
☐ Dove grey

☐ Creamy white
☐ Dark brown
☐ Black

Eyes

☐ Blue with white rays
☐ Clear blue
☐ Steel blue
☐ Green with golden flecks
☐ Clear green
☐ Aqua
☐ Teal
☐ Golden brown

Typical Spring Colours

The Spring palette is warm, light and bright. You do not wear dark or heavy colours well, so strive for medium-dark to light shades. Avoid muted, greyish colours, as you will look washed-out in them.

Most Springs have high colour in their cheeks and therefore wear all their colours well. If you are a very fair, blonde Spring, you will find that your yellow and yellow-green are too strong if large areas of either are worn. If you are a dark-haired Spring, you may find that your camel and pastel colours look best when mixed with a more vivid colour. They will not be your best neutrals. The true greys of Winter will be excellent replacements.

Ivory (White)

Your best white is ivory, a creamy white. You may also wear Summer's soft white, but not Winter's pure white, which will make you look pale. The soft white is especially important for the dark-haired Spring.

Grey

Your greys must be clear and warm with yellow undertones, and have a bright, crisp quality. Light and medium greys are your best. A medium or light true grey will work well for the dark-haired Spring. Occasionally a dark-haired Spring looks good in charcoal grey or black.

Blue

Your most flattering navy is a light, bright one. The next best is a darker but still bright and clear navy. Your other blues range from a light true blue to periwinkle blue, or those with a violet tone. Your aquas and turquoise are plentiful, ranging from medium to bright. A light clear blue is good on a Spring. Avoid any blue that is too pale or powdered. You look best in blues with depth or brightness.

Browns and Beige

Your beiges and browns range from ivory to clear, warm beige to golden tan, camel and medium golden brown. Be sure to avoid wearing any muted or muddy browns, such as khaki, next to your face, though you can wear khaki trousers or skirts. Some Springs will be better using the browns and camels as accents and using the greys of Winter or Summer instead.

Gold and Yellow

Your gold is light and clear. Buff and chamois colours are very good on you, as is bright golden yellow. The bright yellow gold of Autumn is excellent on some Springs.

Red

The Spring woman's reds are either orange-reds or clear reds. Darker reds are harsh and ageing to your face, so they should be avoided. Some Springs may also wear light rust. Others are better in the true reds of Winter.

Greens

Yellow greens range from pastel to bright. They are often too bright for the light Spring.

Pink and Peach

All shades of peach, apricot, coral, salmon and warm pink are for you. You do not have to be at all careful when choosing clothes in this colour family. You wear them from light shades to medium and bright ones.

Warm pinks have yellow in them, easy to see when compared to blue-pink. Some true bright pinks can also be worn by dark-haired Springs.

Orange

Your orange is fairly light; never as bright as Autumn's orange.

Violet

Medium violet is your version of purple. Avoid darker purples; they will look too harsh with your colouring.

ARE YOU MORE THAN ONE SEASON?

Your genes determine your skin tone, hair colour and eye colour, which in turn determine the colours that look best on you. The right colours smooth and clarify your face, minimise shadows and circles under the eyes and make wrinkles or lines at the side of the mouth and nose blend smoothly into your face. They bring out a healthy glow in your skin and make your eyes sparkle. Your face stands out, pushing the colours into the background; the right colours harmonise with your face.

The wrong colours make your face look pale, sallow or dirty; they will accentuate wrinkles, lines or shadows under the eyes, as well as any blotches or scars. They may age your face, especially if you are over thirty. The colours will look too strong or too weak, in either case making your face fade into the background. They do not harmonise with your face.

Your genetically determined skin tone does not change in summer; it simply darkens with a tan or fades somewhat with age. Nor does your season change if your hair goes grey, though you may prefer to wear the lighter and softer colours from your palette. Your most flattering neutral colours will be those that harmonise with your hair – your season's greys and blues.

Most people can find a seasonal group of colours that is best for them. However, some colours in the palette will not be as good as others. It is therefore necessary to add colours from another palette that best describe your individual characteristics.

By understanding the flow of colours from one season to another, you will be able to expand your seasonal palette and still create a co-ordinated wardrobe.

Here are some typical questions and answers about your colours and seasons.

QUESTION: I am a Winter, but I always get compliments when I wear colours from the Autumn palette. How is this possible?

ANSWER: Some Autumn colours are closely related to the Winter palette – those that are deep and not particularly golden. They can be handsome additions to your Winter palette and still allow correct co-ordination of your wardrobe.

QUESTION: I have been analysed by two qualified colour consultants. I was told by one that I was a Summer and by the other that I was an Autumn. Which am I?

ANSWER: It is possible for you to have some of the characteristics of both seasons. Your colouring is obviously soft and muted, since both Summer and Autumn colours are muted.

QUESTION: I'm getting bored with my colours. I would like more individuality in my selection and use of colour. What should I do?

ANSWER: There are hundreds of possibilities within your colours, which were given to you as a guide. Any colours that are obviously related to these will also be in your palette.

THE THREE FACETS
OF COLOUR

Within each of the palettes there are three clearly definable characteristics: *undertone, depth* and *clarity*.

The undertone of a colour is the base tone, which is either gold or blue. You will see the difference in virtually all colours; compare blue-green and yellow-green, blue-red, and orange-red and royal blue and teal blue. Some colours are known as true colours; they have equal amounts of blue and gold in the base. Compare blue-red, true red and orange-red and notice the change from blue base to gold base.

The depth of a colour refers to how dark or light it is. By adding white to red you get pink, and by adding black you get maroon. Both pink and maroon are different intensities of red. It is sometimes easier to think of a scale from white to black with ten steps of grey in between. Each step is a different depth.

The clarity of a colour is often the most difficult characteristic to see. Its clarity is defined by how bright or soft a colour is. To soften a colour, grey is added. The effect is muted, which is often known as 'greyed down'. There are fourteen possible steps in considering clarity of colour at various levels of intensity. Some colours are less bright than others. Red can be made much brighter than blue-green. Each colour has its own clarity range. The important thing to note is that some are bright and others are soft and muted; the *degree* of brightness or softness is not important for our purposes.

In order to clearly see the relationship between all colours, and subsequently their relationship to you, it is easier to look at one characteristic at a time. I will start by considering the relationship between colours that have the same base tone. The Autumn and Spring colours, which have a gold base, are referred to as the 'warm' colours. Look at the Autumn/Spring flow chart on pages 112–113. The colours are arranged from the deepest and most muted of the Autumn colours to the lightest and clearest of the Spring. There is a gradual movement of each colour from one end of the chart to the other. Notice, especially, the colours in the centre band (the right side of the Autumn chart and the left side of the Spring chart) and their similarities.

The 'cool' colours of Winter and Summer have a blue base tone. In the Winter/Summer flow chart on pages 110–111 the colours are arranged from the deepest, brightest, and most vivid of Winter to the lightest and most muted of Summer. The colours in the centre band are very closely related. Notice the gradual flow from the dark to the light colours, all with the same base tone.

It is interesting to discover that in both the warm and cool flow charts there is no obvious line of demarcation, where one season stops and the other begins, but rather a gradual movement and flow from one season to the next. As we continue analysing the other characteristics, the same phenomenon will be seen.

Seeing red about red

I am always amazed when I hear people say with total conviction that they 'can't wear red'. There are so many shade intensities of red that this is a meaningless statement unless you specify which red.

Colour expert Albert Munsell, in his study of the characteristics of colour, noted that the depth of a colour is its most dominant characteristic – the one that is noticed first. As we continue our study of colours, it is therefore important to look at colours that are so related.

The Winter/Autumn flow chart (pages 114–115) contains deep, rich colours that are arranged from the brightest and 'bluest' of Winter to the most muted and golden of Autumn. Both Autumn and Winter colours are deep in intensity. The colours in the centre band of the chart have almost equal amounts of gold and blue and cannot be described as either very golden or very blue. Overall, the Summer/Spring flow chart (pages 116–117) contains light colours as compared with the Winter/Autumn chart. The colours are arranged from the most blue and muted of Summer to the most golden and clear of Spring. Notice that the colours in the centre band are so closely related that some are almost interchangeable.

The final characteristic of colour must not be ignored, in spite of the fact that it is less obvious than either the undertone or the intensity. The degree of *clarity* of a colour makes a tremendous impact. Consider the difference between a bright, vivid magenta and a soft rose. As you add grey to the magenta, you will soften it so that it begins to resemble the soft rose. The current popularity of 'neon' colours epitomises the clarity of colour.

It is important to compare colours that are related in terms of clarity. The Summer and Autumn palettes both contain muted colours. The Summer/Autumn flow chart colours (pages 118–119) are arranged from the most blue of Summer to the most golden of Autumn. The centre band contains muted colours that are very closely related.

The last flow chart contains bright colours. It is interesting to look at these next to the muted colours of Summer and Autumn. The Winter/Spring flow colours (pages 120–121) have been arranged from the deepest and most blue of Winter to the lightest and most golden of Spring. Notice the true colours in the centre band, which contains colours that are neither too light nor too dark.

It is fascinating to look at the flow charts carefully and to understand that all colours are related to each other in a smooth continuous flow. The depth, clarity and base tone of the colours do not change drastically within a season or between seasons.

In addition to the flow from one season to the next, some colours have characteristics that allow them to appear in several flow chart bands. They are the emerald turquoise of Spring, the periwinkle blues, the bright warm pink of Spring, the soft white of Summer, the true grey of Winter and the soft rose of Summer.

As we worked towards finding the styles that are best for you, we looked at the characteristics of clothing that correspond to the same characteristics of your body, i.e. line and scale. To determine which colours are most complimentary to you, we must do the same thing. Now we have looked at the base tone, depth and clarity of colours, we must look at these same characteristics as they apply to your colouring.

THE EXPANDED COLOUR SYSTEM

Some of you may have difficulty in trying to decide which specific season best describes your colouring. You may have recognised some characteristics in two of the seasons, both of which apply to you.

For example, during my first colour analysis, it was determined that I was a Spring. For the first year, I wore many of the Spring colours and loved them, but found I was not comfortable in the brightest colours from the palette. During my training to become a colour consultant, it was decided that I actually looked better in the Autumn palette of colours. I knew that my first analysis had not been totally wrong, since I still loved and felt good in some of the Spring colours.

However, not until I discovered the *flow of colours* from season to season did it become clear to me that I had colouring that was best described as Autumn, but that could reach into the Spring palette. As I looked at the skin tone, hair and eye colour charts, I noticed especially that my hair was really more spring-like in colour and that my skin tone is described in the charts of both seasons.

After I saw myself in both seasons, I realised that if I could use colours from another palette successfully, everybody else had this possibility.

I therefore went to work on an expanded system for each palette, believing that if I could logically and realistically expand the system, there would be no limit to the colours we could all wear.

In addition to having a season, each of us can reach in the direction of another season.

As a Winter, you will lean towards: Summer, Autumn or Spring

As a Summer, you will lean towards: Winter, Spring or Autumn

As an Autumn, you will lean towards: Spring, Winter or Summer

As a Spring, you will lean towards: Autumn, Summer or Winter

Determining your new expanded range of colours is very simple. All you need to do is look at the three characteristics of your colouring and determine which one is the most dominant. Once this is known, it is simply a matter of looking at the corresponding flow chart and adding colours from the centre band.

Remember that there are three characteristics to choose from; the undertone, the depth, and the clarity of your colouring. As in looking at the colour palettes, it is easier to look at one characteristic at a time.

When you found your season, you gained an understanding of your colouring. Since each season encompasses the three characteristics, it is important to try to identify the one that is seen when you look at yourself in the mirror.

In each case, you will start with a major seasonal palette and add a direction into a second season which is most like the predominant characteristics of your colouring.

Some of you have obviously golden colouring. If your major characteristic is your 'golden' quality, you will never have been noticed for your hair or dramatic colouring. Instead, you may frequently hear comments like, 'You have a lot of red in your hair', or, 'In the sunlight you look like a redhead'. You may have golden freckles or eyes on which you are constantly complimented because of their golden starbursts and warm burnished tone. A medium golden-brown colour will always look wonderful on you. If the overall impression that you project has a golden glow and a warm undertone, you have determined your major colour characteristic to be golden.

Some of you may have an obvious blue base to your skin tone, as seen in your rosy or pink complexion. You, too, will be neither very dark nor very light, and your hair will have an ash tone. Once your hair begins to grey, you may frequently be asked if you frost it, since it will have a pearly grey tone. Your eyes will have a similar grey tone to them, regardless of whether they are blue or green. If your eyes are brown, they will be ash or coal brown and your skin tone will be very pink. You will look wonderful in all shades of blue. If your colouring is predominantly 'cool', your major characteristic will be your blue-based skin tone.

If you cannot say with certainty that you are either warm or cool, you may have had difficulty determining your major season. You may, in fact, appear to have almost equal amounts of gold and blue base to your colouring.

Are you often described as having strong, vivid, or deep colouring? Do people comment on your dark, exotic eyes? Have you ever been asked if you dye your hair because it has such a deep rich colour? Do you need contrast and depth in clothing colours to complement your colouring? Since *depth* is the first characteristic that is noticed by the human eye, you should find it easy to decide if your major characteristic is the depth of your colouring.

If your colouring is not deep and strong, you might often have been described as fair, light, or even delicate. Your most frequent compliment may be about your beautiful natural blonde hair. You may often get special attention in public places because your colouring is so light and fragile. Your dark-haired friend will usually have to carry her own suitcase in the airport, while several gentlemen offer to carry yours. You will look wonderful in shades of pink, including the warm pinks. Your dominant characteristic is your light colouring. Often what is most striking is the *depth* of your colouring.

If you are not obviously warm or cool, and if you cannot say with certainty that you are light or dark, your dominant characteristic will have to do with the *clarity* of your colouring. The first thing that you may be able to notice about yourself is that you have a very soft, muted look. In this case, your colouring will definitely be in the medium range with respect to depth. Bright colours will look garish on you and you will find that your best colours are the most greyish ones. People will often comment on the softness of your look. Your dominant characteristic will be your muted colouring.

Those of you who have been unable to identify your major characteristic so far probably have very bright, clear colouring. You will find that your skin tone is light, whether it is ivory or porcelain. Your hair is dark in comparison with your skin tone and your eyes are clear and bright, like jewels. You will find that you are most comfortable in the true colours and that you come to life in bright colours. Your most frequent compliment will be about your bright look or 'porcelain' complexion. Your dominant characteristic will be your bright colouring.

Look back to the charts on pages 70–85 describing skin tone, hair, and eye colouring and once again try to identify the one group that best describes your colouring. As you begin to home-in on your own colouring and its characteristics you will better understand your colours. Look also at the pictures of the models on pages 101–107 and notice the similarities and differences within each season and from one season to the next. The seasons combine as follows:

—Winter and Summer colouring – Blue (cool) undertone
—Autumn and Spring colouring – Golden (warm) undertone
—Winter and Autumn colouring – Deep intensity
—Summer and Spring colouring – Light intensity
—Summer and Autumn colouring – Muted clarity
—Winter and Spring colouring – Bright clarity

SELECTING THE RIGHT FLOW CHART

Once you have determined which characteristic of your colouring is the dominant one, select the right flow chart to determine your best range of colours. The flow charts are simply arranged by the three characteristics; undertone, depth and clarity.

Start with your season and add colours from the centre band of the flow chart on pages 110–121 that best describes your dominant characteristic. These colours will be closely related to those from your major season. Alternatively, you may start at the centre band and move out in the direction that best describes your colouring and in which you feel most comfortable. Your personal likes and dislikes are very important.

Let's now look at the flow charts and the colours in the centre bands of each to analyse more closely how they are related and to show you why you will be able to expand your palette.

In the cool chart of Winter/Summer, the colours are arranged from the deepest and most vivid of Winter to the softest and most muted of Summer. Notice the colours in the centre band. The soft white of Summer can be worn successfully by everyone. The medium greys of Winter and the blue-greys of Summer are in the same range. The charcoal grey of Winter becomes the black of the centre band colours. The blues in the Winter flow section are the true blue and the navy. However, the navy will not be as deep as it is in the true Winter palette. The periwinkle of Summer is added, in spite of the fact that it is lighter than the other band colours, because it is clear enough to work well. The greens and yellows are closely related. The medium pinks of Winter and the rose pink of Summer appear to be almost interchangeable. The deep rose of Summer is a little more muted than some of the other band colours, but the depth and richness make it right. The burgundies, blue-reds and raspberry are truly flow colours. The plum, orchid and fuchsia of Summer are medium to dark in intensity and the clearest of the Summer colours.

In the warm chart of Autumn/Spring, the colours are arranged from the deepest and most muted of Autumn to the lightest and clearest of Spring. Look at the colours in the centre band. The oyster, beige and camel of Autumn are very similar to the ivory and tans of Spring. The yellow-gold, terracotta and pumpkin of Autumn are light and clear enough not to appear too heavy next to Spring's light clear gold and golden brown. The salmon and peach of Autumn, although more muted than the salmon and peach of Spring, are still light enough to be in the same range. The orange-reds of Autumn and Spring are essentially interchangeable. It is possible to include the bittersweet of Autumn in this centre band. The greens included from both palettes are bright and clear. The teals, turquoises and aquas of each season are as clearly related as the beiges. The periwinkle and purple of Autumn are only slightly deeper than Spring's periwinkle and violet, but are clear and light enough to be in the flow range.

In the deep chart of Winter/Autumn, the colours are arranged from the deepest and bluest of Winter to the most muted and golden of Autumn. Look at the centre band colours. Notice that the deep brown of Autumn is very dark, not particularly golden, and works well with black accessories. Black and charcoal are included in the flow band as neutrals. The mahogany is a cross between rust and burgundy and therefore fits appropriately in the band. Because some rusts are clear and contain more red than orange, that rust is included. To oyster and taupe, Summer's soft white can be added. The turquoise and Chinese blue of Winter contain yellow in the base and are appropriately included. The teal and turquoise of Autumn create a blue-green effect. The periwinkle is blue and clear enough to be worn with the Winter colours. The true greens of Winter and the pine green are obviously similar to the forest green of Autumn. The olive is the most muted but the intensity and the 'grey' effect make it work. The true red of Winter has equal amounts of gold and blue and therefore is directly related to the tomato red of Autumn. The purples are almost interchangeable in the intensity comparison.

In the light chart of Summer/Spring, the colours are arranged from the bluest of Summer to the most golden of Spring. Again, observe the centre band. The ivory and buff of Spring are yellow-based but clear.

The soft white and light lemon yellow are clear and blend well with the Spring palette. The blue-greens of Summer contain yellow and are clear enough to work with the Spring band colours. The pinks of Spring are warm with a hint of yellow, and therefore look very similar to the true pinks of Summer. The deep rose is the darkest colour in the band, but it has a slight warm tone. The light true red of Spring contains both blue and gold. The watermelon of Summer actually has a touch of coral in it, and is often referred to as Summer's orange. Spring's emerald turquoise is blue-green and is therefore closely related to the blue-green of Summer. The turquoises do not have a strong yellow base. Any periwinkle is compatible with both seasons and cannot be omitted. The medium blue of Summer and the light clear navy of Spring are similar and not too dark to be included in the band. The medium true grey of Winter is an excellent colour to be added to the centre band, since it is not too deep and does not contain an excess of blue. It is a wonderful flow colour for both seasons.

The same gradual flow from one season to the next, which was obvious in the warm and cool flow charts, is also apparent on the intensity flow charts of Winter/Autumn and Summer/Spring. Once again, there is no definitive line of demarcation.

In the muted chart of Summer/Autumn, the colours are arranged from the bluest of Summer to the most golden of Autumn. Look at the band colours and notice the browns. The Autumn browns are neither too dark nor especially golden. They are very similar to the cocoa and rose-brown of Summer. The soft white and oyster are closely related; the oyster is a little deeper. The mohogany of Autumn is a muted brown-burgundy and it works with many colours in the Summer band. As it becomes more soft and muted, it becomes a better flow colour. The greens of Autumn are soft, muted, and greyish, with an almost pastel quality. The forest green is a bit dark, but as it is greyed down, it works well as a flow colour. The blue-greens of Summer are the yellowest of the Summer colours and work with the many greens of Autumn. The salmon of Autumn has a warm pink tone, as does the rose of Summer. The rose pink and the deep rose are soft and muted. The bittersweet of Autumn is muted, not too deep or golden. The watermelon of Summer has a touch of coral and works well, as it did in the Summer/Spring chart. The periwinkles are interchangeable, as they are in most of the charts. The teal of Autumn is muted and is blue-green in tone. The more muted it is, the better it will be as a flow colour. The turquoises included are muted, not exceptionally golden.

In the bright chart of Winter/Spring, the colours have been arranged from the deepest and bluest of Winter to the lightest and most golden of Spring. Notice the centre band colours. The ivory and taupe are closely related. Since the ivory is often very golden, substituting the oyster of Autumn or the soft white of Summer are excellent options. The light and medium greys of Winter are true colours, which are not too dark and which work beautifully as flow neutrals. The warm grey is clear enough to be included with the greys of Winter. The true blues of both seasons are closely related, as are the yellows. The true greens work in the band, as do all the true colours. The hot turquoise and Chinese blue of Winter both contain some yellow and work well with the turquoise of Spring. The bright warm pinks of Spring are bright enough to be included, and the shocking pink and deep hot pink of Winter are true pinks. The true reds and purples of each palette are almost the same.

Cool Band Colours

Winter	*Summer*
Light True Grey	Soft White
True Grey	Light Blue-Grey
Charcoal Grey	Charcoal Blue-Grey
Taupe	Rose-Beige
Royal Blue	Cocoa
Navy	Periwinkle Blue
Light True Green	Medium Blue
Lemon Yellow	Greyish Navy
Shocking Pink	Deep Blue-Green
Deep Hot Pink	Light Lemon Yellow
Bright Burgundy	Deep Rose
Blue-Red	Rose Pink
Royal Purple	Burgundy
	Blue-Red
	Raspberry
	Plum
	Orchid
	Soft Fuchsia

Warm Band Colours

Autumn	*Spring*
Oyster White	Ivory
Warm Beige	Buff
Camel	Light Warm Beige
Yellow-Gold	Camel
Gold	Light Clear Gold
Pumpkin	Golden Tan
Orange	Medium Golden Brown
Terracotta	Peach
Deep Peach/Apricot	Apricot
Salmon	Light Orange
Orange-Red	Orange-Red
Bright Yellow-Green	Bright Yellow-Green
Turquoise	Light Warm Aqua
Teal Blue	Clear Bright Aqua
Deep Periwinkle Blue	Emerald Turquoise
Purple	Light Periwinkle Blue
	Dark Periwinkle Blue
	Medium Violet

Deep Band Colours

Winter	*Autumn*
Charcoal Grey	Mahogany
Black	Dark Chocolate Brown
Lemon Yellow	Rust
Taupe	Oyster White
Hot Turquoise	Turquoise
Chinese Blue	Teal Blue
True Blue	Deep Periwinkle Blue
Light True Green	Forest Green
True Green	Olive Green
Pine Green	Dark Tomato Red
True Red	Purple
Royal Purple	

Light Band Colours

Summer	*Spring*
Soft White	Ivory
Light Lemon Yellow	Buff
Medium Blue-Green	Camel
Deep Blue-Green	Warm Pastel Pink
Powder Pink	Coral Pink
Rose Pink	Clear Bright Warm Pink
Deep Rose	Clear Salmon
Watermelon	Clear Bright Red
Pastel Aqua	Emerald Turquoise
Periwinkle Blue	Clear Bright Aqua
Sky Blue	Light Periwinkle Blue
Medium Blue	Dark Periwinkle Blue
Light Blue-Grey	Light Clear Navy
Charcoal Blue-Grey	Light Warm Grey

Muted Band Colours

Summer	*Autumn*
Soft White	Oyster White
Rose-Beige	Coffee Brown
Cocoa	Mahogany
Rose-Brown	Greyish Green
Light Lemon Yellow	Jade Green
Medium Blue-Green	Olive Green
Deep Blue-Green	Forest Green
Deep Rose	Salmon
Rose Pink	Bittersweet
Watermelon	Deep Periwinkle Blue
Periwinkle Blue	Turquoise
Pastel Aqua	Teal Blue
Grey-Blue	

Bright Band Colours

Winter	*Spring*
Taupe	Ivory
Light True Grey	Light Warm Grey
True Grey	Light Clear Navy
True Blue	Light True Blue
Lemon Yellow	Dark Periwinkle Blue
Light True Green	Bright Golden Yellow
True Green	Emerald Turquoise
Hot Turquoise	Clear Bright Aqua
Chinese Blue	Coral Pink
Shocking Pink	Clear Bright Warm Pink
Deep Hot Pink	Clear Bright Red
True Red	Medium Violet
Royal Purple	

REACHING INTO
ANOTHER SEASON

To establish your new expanded range of colours, I have explained how you should first identify your major seasonal palette and then add colours from a second seasonal palette which also contains your predominant characteristic – undertone (cool/warm), depth (deep/light) or clarity (muted/bright). Now take a good look at the photographs that follow and see how the colouring of the models differs within the same major season. Once you have identified your season or dominant characteristic, turn to the relevant flow chart and discover the full range of colours that will suit you best.

WINTER

Colours for an Expanded Wardrobe

WINTER → Summer
The Soft Fuchsia is blue-based and deep enough for the Winter/Summer to wear successfully.

WINTER → Autumn
The Teal Blue has the right intensity and a blue-green tone. It therefore works well for the Winter/Autumn.

WINTER → Spring
The Emerald Turquoise is a bright clear colour with a blue-green quality. It looks fabulous on the Winter/Spring.

Soft Fuchsia (Summer)   *Teal Blue* (Autumn)   *Emerald Turquoise* (Spring)

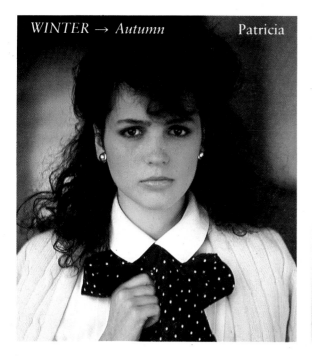

WINER → *Autumn*   Patricia

WINTER → *Summer*   Susan

WINTER → *Spring*   Joan

WINTER → *Autumn*

Patricia has deep colouring. Her dark brown eyes have a hint of green in them, and she has dark brunette hair. Since her skin tone is blue, the muted and most golden of the autumn colours are not her best.

WINTER → *Summer*

Susan has a clean complexion. Her eyes are grey-blue and her hair is medium brown. Her cool colouring is neither very dark nor very light. This cool undertone is her most dominant characteristic. She has colouring similar to that of some Summers.

WINTER → *Spring*

Joan has porcelain skin, brunette hair and bright hazel eyes. Her dominant colour characteristic is her brightness. She has colouring similar to that of some Springs.

SUMMER

Colours for an Expanded Wardrobe

SUMMER → Winter
The Deep Hot Pink is not too bright for a Summer/Winter to wear. It is medium in intensity and very flattering.

SUMMER → Autumn
The Greyed Green has a soft, muted look with very little yellow. It has a pastel-like quality and therefore looks wonderful on the Summer/Autumn.

SUMMER → Spring
The Clear Bright Aqua does not have a predominance of yellow and looks exciting on the Summer/Spring.

| Deep Hot Pink (Winter) | Greyed Green (Autumn) | Clear Bright Aqua (Spring) |

SUMMER → Winter   Laurie

SUMMER → Autumn   Valerie

SUMMER → Spring   Sue

SUMMER → Winter
Laurie's natural hair colour is a medium ash brown. She has a rosy complexion and deep blue eyes. Her cool colouring is deeper and brighter than that of many Summers.

SUMMER → Autumn
Valerie also has medium ash brown hair. However, her eyes are a soft, blue-green. Her complexion is not as obviously cool as Laurie's. Her dominant characteristic is her muted colouring, like that of some Autumns.

SUMMER → Spring
Sue's colouring is light. She has light blonde hair with some warm highlights and soft blue eyes. Her complexion is cool, but similar to that of a Spring.

AUTUMN

Colours for an Expanded Wardrobe

AUTUMN → Winter
True Red is a deep colour that complements the Autumn/Winter person.

AUTUMN → Summer
Deep Blue-Green has enough yellow in it and is the right intensity for the Autumn/Summer person.

AUTUMN → Spring
The Light Clear Gold is very golden and soft enough to look special on the Autumn/Spring.

True Red (Winter)   *Deep Blue-Green* (Summer)   *Light Clear Gold* (Spring)

AUTUMN → Winter Sandy

AUTUMN → Summer Judy

AUTUMN → Spring Jennifer

AUTUMN → Winter

Sandy has ivory skin, dark warm brown eyes, and deep auburn hair. The depth of her colouring is her dominant characteristic. She has colouring similar to that of some Winters.

AUTUMN → Summer

Judy has medium golden blonde hair and green eyes. Her colouring is neither very dark nor very light. Her dominant characteristic is the softness of her colouring, which is similar to that of some Summers.

AUTUMN → Spring

Jennifer has auburn hair, blue-green eyes and a golden complexion. Her dominant characteristic is her warm undertone. She has golden colouring similar to that of some Springs.

SPRING

Colours for an Expanded Wardrobe

SPRING →Autumn
The Pumpkin of Autumn is light and bright enough to complement the Spring/Autumn.

SPRING → Summer
The Watermelon has a slight touch of Coral and is often referred to as the 'orange' of Summer. It is thus a wonderful Spring/Summer colour.

SPRING → Winter
The Chinese Blue is bright and clear with enough yellow in it to look fabulous on the Spring/Winter.

Pumpkin   *Watermelon*   *Chinese*
(Autumn)   (Summer)   *Blue*
                                       (Winter)

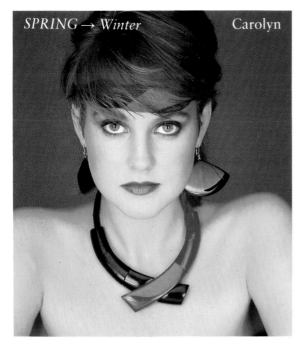

SPRING → *Winter*　　　　　Carolyn

SPRING → *Autumn*　　　　Sharon

SPRING → *Winter*

Carolyn has mid brown hair and bright, clear blue-grey eyes. Her ivory complexion is very bright and is in strong contrast to her hair. The brightness of her colouring is her most dominant characteristic. She has colouring similar to that of some Winters.

SPRING → *Autumn*

Sharon has warm golden hair, green eyes and golden skin. Her most dominant characteristic is her golden colouring, which is similar to that of many Autumns.

SPRING → *Summer*

Marie's colouring is light. She has a warm pink complexion, light golden blonde hair and warm blue eyes. Her colouring is similar to that of some Summers.

SPRING → *Summer*　　　　Marie

TESTING YOUR COLOUR CHOICES

If you are still having difficulty in finding your dominant characteristic, or if you would like to test your selection, you may try some test colours. Since you have already identified your season, look at the three flow charts that contain your season and compare colours from the centre band of these charts.

If you are an **Autumn**, to determine or confirm your flow chart, try:

Autumn/Spring	*Autumn/Summer*	*Autumn/Winter*
Bright Yellow-Green	Deep Blue-Green	True Green
Orange-Red	Watermelon	True Red
Medium Golden Brown	Cocoa	Charcoal

If you are a **Spring**, to determine or confirm your flow, try:

Spring/Autumn	*Spring/Summer*	*Spring/Winter*
Teal Blue	Medium Blue	True Blue
Orange-Red	Watermelon	True Red
Bright Yellow-Green	Medium Blue-Green	True Green

If you are a **Summer**, to determine or confirm your flow, try:

Summer/Winter	*Summer/Autumn*	*Summer/Spring*
Deep Hot Pink	Salmon	Warm Pink
Light True Green	Greyish Green	Emerald Turquoise
Royal Blue	Teal Blue	Light Clear Navy

If you are a **Winter**, to determine or confirm your flow, try:

Winter/Autumn	*Winter/Summer*	*Winter/Spring*
Teal Blue	Medium Blue	Light True Blue
Dark Tomato Red	Blue-Red	Clear Bright Red
Forest Green	Deep Blue-Green	Emerald Turquoise

One of the three sets of flow colours will look better on you than the others. These colours and their flow chart will confirm your flow season.

HOW TO USE COLOUR CHARTS

This is a complete palette of one season's colours.

This is a complete palette of one season's colours.

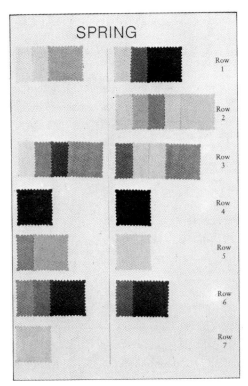

Non-flow Colours
These are colours *not* related to the other season in this chart.

Flow Colours
These are the colours most related to the other season in this chart. These are the **centre band** colours.

Flow Colours
These are the colours most related to the other season in this chart. These are the **centre band** colours.

Non-flow Colours
These are colours *not* related to the other season in this chart.

COOL CHART

Winter/Summer

The colours of the cool chart are arranged from the deepest and most vivid of Winter (*left side page 110*) to the lightest and most muted of Summer (*right side page 111*). The centre band colours *flow* from one palette to the other with no distinct line of demarcation between the two seasons.

Winter Palette

The Winter colours are blue-based, deep and bright.

Row 1   (*L to R*) black, white, charcoal grey, true grey, light true grey

Row 2   (*L to R*) taupe

Row 3   (*L to R*) Chinese blue, hot turquoise, true blue, navy, royal blue

Row 4   (*L to R*) pine green, emerald green, true green, light true green

Row 5   (*L to R*) lemon yellow

Row 6   (*L to R*) fuchsia, magentia, deep hot pink, shocking pink

Row 7   (*L to R*) true red, blue-red, burgundy

Row 8   (*L to R*) icy yellow, aqua, green, blue, violet, pink, royal purple

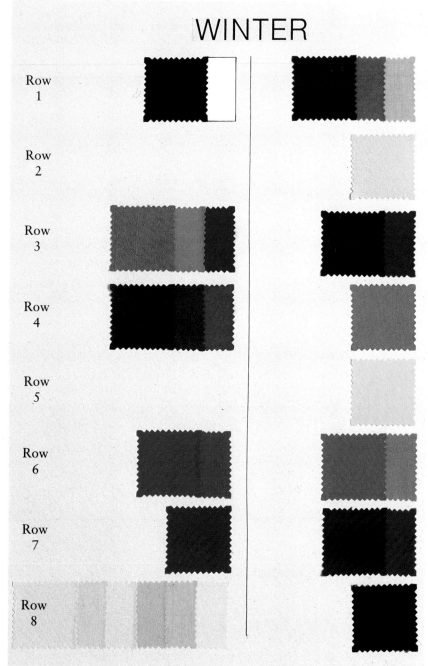

WINTER

Row 1

Row 2

Row 3

Row 4

Row 5

Row 6

Row 7

Row 8

SUMMER

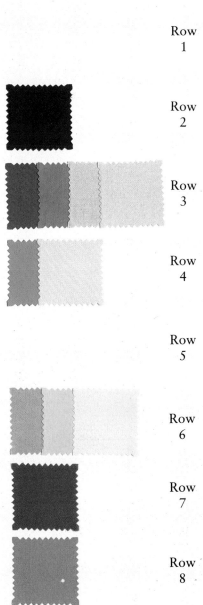

Row 1

Row 2

Row 3

Row 4

Row 5

Row 6

Row 7

Row 8

Summer Palette

The Summer colours are blue-based, light and muted.

Row 1   (*L to R*) soft white, light blue-grey, charcoal blue-grey

Row 2   (*L to R*) rose-beige, cocoa, rose-brown

Row 3   periwinkle blue, medium blue, greyed navy, grey-blue, sky blue, powder blue, pastel aqua

Row 4   (*L to R*) deep blue-green, medium blue-green, pastel blue-green

Row 5   (*L to R*) light lemon yellow

Row 6   (*L to R*) deep rose, rose pink, lavender, powder pink, pastel pink

Row 7   (*L to R*) burgundy, blue-red, raspberry, watermelon

Row 8   (*L to R*) plum, orchid, soft fuchsia, mauve

WARM CHART

Autumn/Spring

The colours of the warm chart are arranged from the deepest and most muted of Autumn (*left side page 112*) to the lightest and brightest of Spring (*right side page 113*). The centre band colours *flow* from one palette to the other with no distinct line of demarcation between the two seasons.

Autumn Palette

The Autumn colours are gold-based, deep, and muted.

Row 1   (*L to R*) medium warm bronze, chocolate brown, mahogany, coffee brown, camel, warm beige, oyster white

Row 2   (*L to R*) rust, mustard, terracotta, orange, pumpkin, gold, yellow-gold

Row 3   (*L to R*) salmon, peach/apricot

Row 4   (*L to R*) tomato red, bittersweet, orange-red

Row 5   (*L to R*) olive, greyed green, moss, lime green, chartreuse, bright yellow-green

Row 6   (*L to R*) forest green, jade green, teal, turquoise

Row 7   (*L to R*) purple, deep periwinkle blue

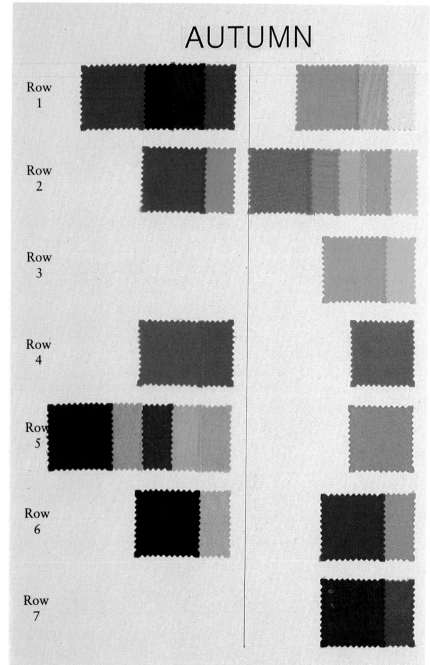

AUTUMN

Row 1

Row 2

Row 3

Row 4

Row 5

Row 6

Row 7

SPRING

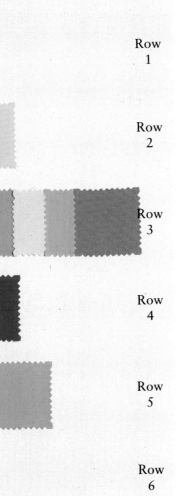

Row 1

Row 2

Row 3

Row 4

Row 5

Row 6

Row 7

Spring Palette

The Spring colours are gold-based, light, and bright.

Row 1 (*L to R*) ivory, buff, light warm beige, camel

Row 2 (*L to R*) light clear gold, golden tan, medium golden brown, bright clear yellow

Row 3 (*L to R*) peach, apricot, light orange, bright coral, clear salmon, warm pastel pink, coral pink, bright clear warm pink

Row 4 (*L to R*) orange-red, light clear red

Row 5 (*L to R*) bright yellow-green, pastel yellow-green, medium yellow-green

Row 6 (*L to R*) light warm aqua, clear bright aqua, emerald turquoise

Row 7 (*L to R*) light periwinkle blue, deep periwinkle blue, medium violet, light clear navy, light true blue, warm grey

DEEP CHART

Winter/Autumn

The colours of the deep chart are arranged from the most blue of Winter (*left side page 114*) to the most golden and muted of Autumn (*right side page 115*). The centre band colours *flow* from one palette to the other with no distinct line of demarcation between the two seasons.

Winter Palette

The Winter colours are blue-based, deep and bright.

Row 1   (*L to R*) white, true grey, light true grey, black, charcoal grey

Row 2   (*L to R*) taupe, lemon, yellow

Row 3   (*L to R*) navy, royal blue, true blue, Chinese blue, hot turquoise

Row 4   (*L to R*) fuchsia, magentia, deep hot pink, shocking pink

Row 5   (*L to R*) emerald green, pine green, true green, light true green

Row 6   (*L to R*) blue-red, burgundy, royal purple, true red

Row 7   (*L to R*) icy pink, violet, blue, aqua, yellow, green

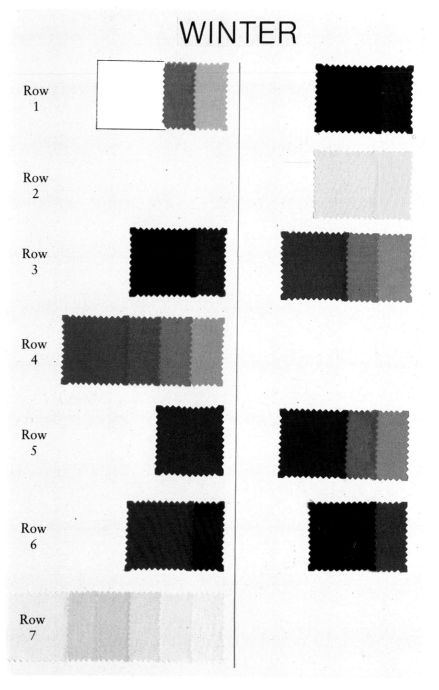

WINTER

Row 1

Row 2

Row 3

Row 4

Row 5

Row 6

Row 7

AUTUMN

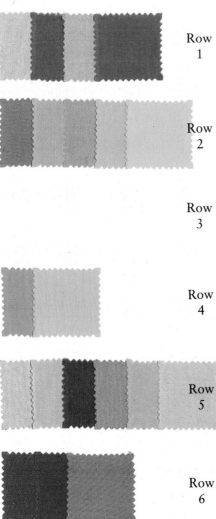

Row 1

Row 2

Row 3

Row 4

Row 5

Row 6

Autumn Palette

The Autumn colours are gold-based, deep, and muted.

Row 1 (*L to R*) mahogany, chocolate brown, rust, warm beige, coffee, brown, camel, medium golden bronze

Row 2 (*L to R*) oyster white, terracotta, pumpkin, mustard, gold, bright yellow-gold

Row 3 (*L to R*) turquoise, teal, deep periwinkle

Row 4 (*L to R*) salmon, peach/apricot

Row 5 (*L to R*) pine green, olive green, jade, greyed green, moss green, bright yellow-green, chartreuse, lime green

Row 6 (*L to R*) tomato red, purple, bittersweet, orange-red, orange

LIGHT CHART

Summer/Spring

The colours of the light chart are arranged from the deepest and most blue of Summer (*left side page 116*) to the most golden of Spring (*right side page 117*). The centre band colours *flow* from one palette to the other with no distinct line of demarcation between the two seasons.

Summer Palette

The Summer colours are blue-based, light and muted.

Row 1 (*L to R*) rose brown, cocoa, rose-beige, soft white
Row 2 (*L to R*) pastel blue-green, deep blue-green, medium blue-green, light lemon yellow
Row 3 (*L to R*) soft fuchsia, mauve, orchid, lavender, pastel pink, deep rose, rose pink, powder pink
Row 4 (*L to R*) plum, burgundy, raspberry, blue-red, watermelon
Row 5 (*L to R*) pastel aqua
Row 6 (*L to R*) greyed navy, grey-blue, powder blue, medium blue, sky blue, periwinkle blue
Row 7 (*L to R*) charcoal blue-grey, light blue-grey

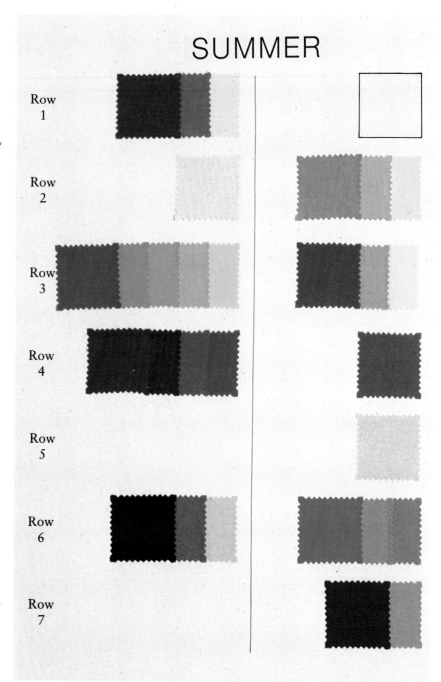

SUMMER

Row 1

Row 2

Row 3

Row 4

Row 5

Row 6

Row 7

SPRING

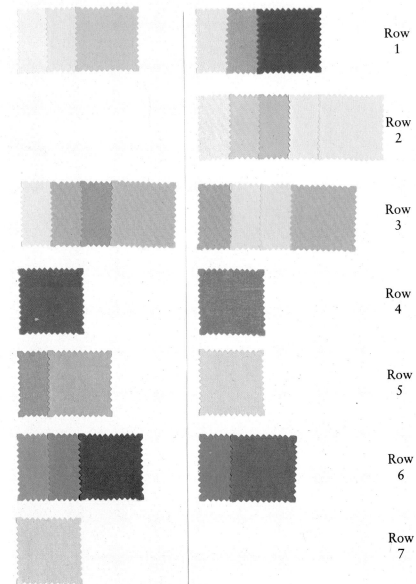

Row 1

Row 2

Row 3

Row 4

Row 5

Row 6

Row 7

Spring Palette

The Spring colours are gold-based, light and bright.

Row 1   (*L to R*) ivory, buff, camel, light warm beige, golden tan, medium golden brown

Row 2   (*L to R*) pastel yellow-green, medium yellow-green, deep yellow-green, light clear gold, bright golden yellow

Row 3   (*L to R*) warm pastel pink, coral pink, clear bright warm pink, clear salmon, bright coral, peach, apricot, light orange

Row 4   (*L to R*) light clear red, orange-red

Row 5   (*L to R*) emerald turquoise, clear bright aqua, light warm aqua

Row 6   (*L to R*) light periwinkle blue, deep periwinkle blue, light clear navy, light true blue, medium violet

Row 7   (*L to R*) light warm grey

MUTED CHART

Summer/Autumn

The colours of the muted chart are arranged from the deepest and most blue of Summer (*left side page 118*) to the most golden of Autumn (*right side page 119*). The centre band colours *flow* from one palette to the other with no distinct line of demarcation between the two seasons.

Summer Palette

The Summer colours are blue-based, light and muted.

Row 1   (*L to R*) charcoal blue-grey, light blue-grey, rose brown, cocoa, rose beige, soft white

Row 2   (*L to R*) light lemon yellow

Row 3   (*L to R*) pastel blue-green, deep blue-green, medium blue-green

Row 4   (*L to R*) soft fuchsia, mauve, orchid, lavender, powder pink, pastel pink, rose pink, deep rose

Row 5   (*L to R*) plum, burgundy, raspberry, blue-red, watermelon

Row 6   (*L to R*) greyed navy, medium blue, sky blue, powder blue, grey-blue, pastel aqua, periwinkle blue

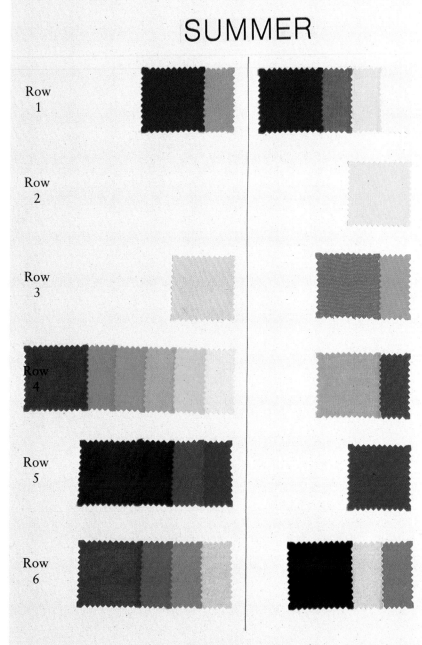

SUMMER

Row 1

Row 2

Row 3

Row 4

Row 5

Row 6

AUTUMN

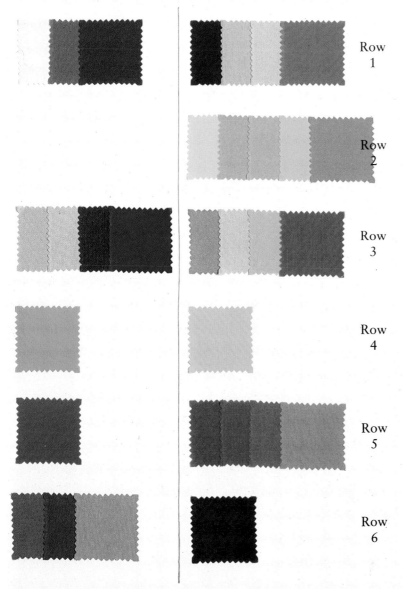

Row 1

Row 2

Row 3

Row 4

Row 5

Row 6

Autumn Palette

The Autumn colours are gold-based, deep and muted.

Row 1 (*L to R*) oyster white, coffee brown, mahogany, chocolate brown, camel, warm beige, medium golden bronze

Row 2 (*L to R*) bright yellow-gold, mustard, pumpkin, gold, terracotta

Row 3 (*L to R*) greyed green, jade, olive, pine green, bright yellow-green, lime green, chartreuse, moss green

Row 4 (*L to R*) salmon, peach/apricot,

Row 5 (*L to R*) bittersweet, rust, tomato red, orange-red

Row 6 (*L to R*) deep periwinkle blue, teal, turquoise, purple

BRIGHT CHART

Winter/Spring

The colours of the bright chart are arranged from the deepest and most blue of Winter (*left side page 120*) to the lightest and most golden of Spring (*right side page 121*). The centre band colours *flow* from one palette to the other with no distinct line of demarcation between the two seasons.

Winter Palette

The Winter colours are blue-based, deep and bright.

Row 1   (*L to R*) white, taupe

Row 2   (*L to R*) black, charcoal grey, true grey, light true grey

Row 3   (*L to R*) navy, royal blue, true blue

Row 4   (*L to R*) pine green, emerald green, true green, light true green, lemon yellow

Row 5   (*L to R*) Chinese blue, hot turquoise

Row 6   (*L to R*) fuchsia, magenta, deep hot pink, shocking pink

Row 7   (*L to R*) burgundy, blue-red, true red

Row 8   (*L to R*) icy green, yellow, blue, pink, lavender, royal purple

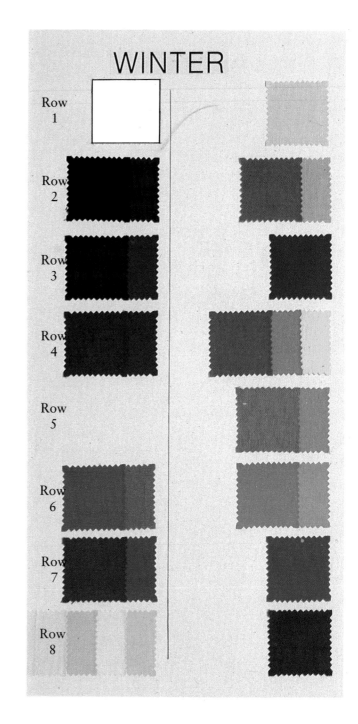

WINTER

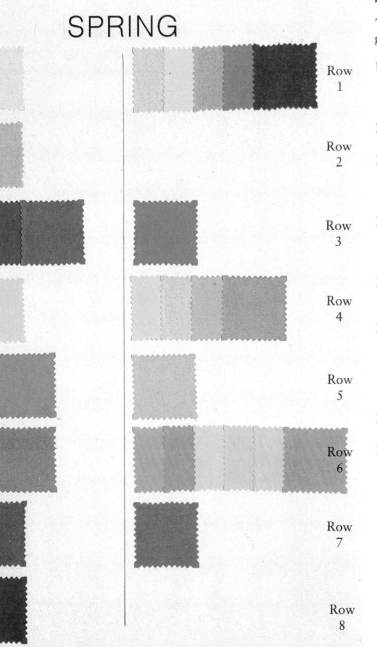

SPRING

Row 1
Row 2
Row 3
Row 4
Row 5
Row 6
Row 7
Row 8

Spring Palette

The Spring colours are gold-based, light and bright.

Row 1 (*L to R*) ivory, warm beige, buff, camel, golden tan, medium golden brown

Row 2 (*L to R*) light warm grey

Row 3 (*L to R*) light clear navy, light true blue, deep periwinkle, light periwinkle

Row 4 (*L to R*) bright golden yellow, light clear gold, pastel yellow-green, bright yellow-green

Row 5 (*L to R*) emerald turquoise, clear bright aqua, light warm aqua

Row 6 (*L to R*) coral pink, clear bright warm pink, clear salmon, bright coral, warm pastel pink, apricot, peach, light orange

Row 7 (*L to R*) light clear red, orange-red

Row 8 (*L to R*) medium violet

DIFFERENT SKIN TYPES

As you can see, seasonal colouring may be extremely varied. Here is a summary of the basics for Caucasians, blacks and Asians.

CAUCASIANS		
Skin tone	*Hair*	*Eye colour*
Winter: blue base, deep, bright Olive Beige White with pink Rose beige Charcoal freckles	Blue-black Dark brown Medium brown Ash brown Salt and pepper Grey (white)	Black-brown Dark brown Dark blue Hazel Grey-blue Grey-green
Summer: blue base, light, muted Rose beige Beige Light beige Very pink	Dark brown Ash brown Platinum blonde Ash blonde Golden blonde Brown with red	Blue Green Grey-blue Grey-green Aqua Hazel Soft brown
Autumn: gold base, deep, muted Golden beige Copper Beige with golden freckles Ivory Peach	Ash blonde Charcoal black Chestnut Red Golden brown Golden blonde Warm grey	Dark brown Hazel Warm green Golden brown Turquoise Amber Teal
Spring: gold base, light, bright Golden beige Beige with golden freckles Ivory Peach	Dark brown Golden brown Auburn Golden blonde Strawberry blonde Flaxen blonde Warm grey	Clear blue Clear green Aqua Blue-green Amber

BLACKS		
	Skin tone	*Hair*	*Eye colour*
Winter: blue base, deep, bright	Blue-black Dark brown with olive Dark ash brown Dark rose brown	Blue-black Black Brown-black Dark brown White/silver	Black Brown-black Red-brown Brown
Summer: blue base, light, muted	Dark brown Rose brown Grey-brown Cocoa brown	Black Black-brown Dark ash brown Soft brown	Brown-black Red-brown Grey-brown Hazel
Autumn: gold base, deep, muted	Dark golden brown Mahogany Medium golden brown Golden brown with golden freckles Bronze	Black Brown-black Chestnut brown Golden brown Warm grey	Brown-black Golden brown Two-tone brown Hazel
Spring: gold base, light, bright	Medium golden brown Caramel Light bronze Copper Light golden brown with warm freckles	Black Red-brown Medium golden brown Light golden brown	Dark brown Warm brown Topaz Hazel

ASIANS			
	Skin tone	*Hair*	*Eye colour*
Winter: blue base, deep, bright	Olive Taupe Beige White with pink White	Blue-black Black Dark brown Medium brown White/silver	Black Black-brown Red-brown Brown
Summer: blue base, light, muted	Beige Rose beige White with pink Very pink	Dark brown (taupe) Ash brown Soft brown Brown with red cast Soft white	Dark brown Rose brown Soft brown Grey-brown
Autumn: gold base, deep, muted	Beige Golden beige Copper Bronze Ivory Peach	Black Dark brown with red light Chestnut brown Dark brown Medium brown	Dark brown Brown-black Deep golden brown Hazel Two-tone brown
Spring: gold base, light, bright	Warm beige Ivory Peach Rosy peach	Black (rare) Dark warm brown Brown with red Warm brown	Dark brown Golden brown Topaz Hazel

COLOUR AND YOUR PERSONALITY

So far, we have studied colours and their relationship to your physical colouring. It is now time to take your personality into consideration, as well as the psychological effects that colour can have on you.

But first let us consider what colours best express your personality. Some people are comfortable only in the conservative colours from the palette, others are more daring. Each colour chart has conservative as well as bold colours: all will flatter you, but you will be most successful when you interpret your palette to reflect your personality.

Think about your image. Whatever your season, you can project the image you desire; each chart provides you with the opportunity to be authoritative or low key, sophisticated or casual, formal or informal.

Finally, each season can be interpreted so that it reflects your mood. Colours in your palette express any mood on a daily basis or even in yearly trends. You may spend several years in the mood for bright colours and then swing to a wish to wear calm ones.

Some colours have definite effects on people. Red, for instance, is a colour that causes strong reactions. It is often associated with feelings of excitement, power and stimulation, as well as aggression, defiance or competitiveness. The comment 'I can't wear red', however, is meaningless, considering the many shades and intensities of the colour and how often shades of it are found in the various palettes. But the statement means something if you are referring to your personal preferences and the psychological effect that red has on you. You should never wear a colour or a shade about which you feel negative. On the next page is a list of the most common colours, with the positive and negative reactions they have traditionally produced.

THE EFFECTS OF COLOUR		
Colour	*Positive feelings*	*Negative feelings*
Yellow	Sunny Cheerful Optimistic	Egocentric Dishonest Sensational
Cream	Tranquil Quiet Consoling Comfortable Natural	Commonplace Invokes envy Immature
Blue	Serene Calm Comfortable Cool Secure	Depressing Melancholic
Violet	Regal Dignified	Cruel Pompous
Brown	Dependable Realistic	Boring Obstinate
Pink	Soft, calm Sweet Tender	Wishy-washy
White	Pure Innocent Spiritual	Sterile
Grey	Secure Peaceful Protective	Dreary Colourless
Black	Sophisticated	Empty Deathly

FASHION COLOURS

After every one of my colour lectures during the past few years there has always been one woman who objected violently to being limited to a single palette of colours. Mentally stamping her foot, she would defiantly assert, 'I will wear any colour I want to wear!' She was often the one person in the audience who always caught my eye because she made such a strong non-verbal impact through her fashion statement.

In the beginning we learned which lines, scales, prints, and textures of clothing are correct for our body type by looking at our face shape and body shape. We expanded this information upon consideration of our personality to create a wardrobe that projects each of us as individuals. Just as we 'added to' or 'multiplied' information to attain our style, so should we determine our direction with colours to *complete* our style.

Our 'outraged' woman wants to wear any – and every – colour. She understands, perhaps, that some colours look better on her than others, but does not want to be limited to a palette, or to a flow chart. She feels that she is justified, through her strong desire and conviction, to wear any colour, especially the fashion colours. Let's look at how she *can* wear her 'fashion' colours and still look fabulous.

You can wear all colours

Thus far, our discussion of colour has been based on the assumption that we are looking for colours that are naturally in balance and harmony with our colouring. Yet, depending on your personality and the occasion, an unusual effect may sometimes be desired. At these times, balance and harmony may not be your goals.

A Winter with contrast in her colouring may want to soften her overall appearance – perhaps for a romantic evening at home. She can do this by adding a softer colour not found in her palette. The Summer with soft muted colouring may tire of the softness and want to wear bright colours for a fun change. She can use the bright colours to create the excitement she is seeking.

In extreme cases, as evidenced by the 'punk' look, you may choose to wear a single colour that is not related to your colouring at all. The person who is most likely to wear non-complementary colours and styles likes to be noticed and wants the freedom to 'go for it'. She has the personality, physical characteristics and self-understanding to wear the outrageous and to enjoy the look. She now has the knowledge to create her most outrageous look successfully.

The following section contains some useful guidelines for expanding your use of colours. It is always important to start with your seasonal colours. You can then add colours as you are ready, depending on your personality and needs.

How To Wear Fashion Colours That Are Not In Your Palette

Each season, designers focus on distinctive colours and combinations in their collections. It is possible to wear these fashion colours successfully, even though they may not be in your palette or flow chart. The colour must be worn in combination with one from your flow chart or in a print that contains one of your flow chart colours. This colour must emphasise your dominant characteristic.

Some colours are favoured by the major designers as either fashion or classic colours. Fashion colours are likely to change from season to season, while classic colours such as navy blue and grey are available each year. It is easy to combine the classic colours with colours from your flow chart and still be able to wear your correct makeup colours. When wearing a fashion colour, care must be taken to use a combination that allows for complementary makeup.

Below are suggested colour combinations for all types of each season.

Olive

Winters can wear it with Deep Hot Pink, Magenta, Fuchsia, Hot Turquoise, True Blue, Burgundy and Blue-Red

Summers can wear it with Soft Fuchsia, Orchid, Periwinkle Blue and Watermelon

Springs can wear it with Clear Salmon, Peach, Emerald Turquoise, Light Warm Aqua, Light True Blue and Bright Golden Yellow

Beige

Winters can wear it with Black, True Red, Royal Blue, Fuchsia and Royal Purple

Summers can wear it with Plum, Mauve, Burgundy, Rose Pink, Pastel Pink, Medium Blue and Deep Rose

Peach

Winters can wear it with Burgundy, Magenta, Deep Hot Pink and True Red

Summers can wear it with Rose Pink, Mauve, Deep Rose and Watermelon

Camel

Winters can wear it with Royal Purple, Fuchsia, Burgundy, Pine Green, Black, Charcoal Grey and Blue-Red

Summers can wear it with Pastel Pink, Mauve-Burgundy, Charcoal Blue-Grey, Periwinkle and Watermelon

Brown

Winters can wear it with Royal Blue, True Red, White, Light True Grey, Fuchsia, Magenta and Deep Hot Pink

Summers can wear it with Periwinkle, Sky Blue, Medium Blue, Mauve, Orchid and Pastel Aqua

Pink

Autumns can wear it with Mahogany, Rust, Peach and Salmon

Springs can wear it with Orange-Red, Clear Bright Red, Clear Salmon and Bright Coral

Navy

Autumns can wear it with Mahogany, Rust, Terracotta, Tomato Red and Gold

Springs can wear it with Orange-Red, Coral Pink, Bright Yellow-Green and Bright Golden Yellow

Burgundy

Autumns can wear it with Rust, Terracotta, Peach and Tomato Red

Springs can wear it with Clear Bright Warm Pink, Coral Pink, Light Orange, Clear Salmon and Orange-Red

Grey

Autumns can wear it with Tomato Red, Teal, Salmon, Camel, Gold and Terracotta

Springs can wear it with Peach, Clear Salmon, Light Warm Aqua, Buff, Clear Bright Red and Light True Blue

The chart on the next two pages will help you combine the colours from your palette with the most fashionable colours.

FASHION COLOUR COMBINATIONS

Fashion Colour	Winter	Summer	Autumn	Spring
Camel	Burgundy Black Royal Purple Blue-Red Charcoal Fuchsia Pine Green	Soft Burgundy Mauve Charcoal Blue-Grey Pastel Pink Periwinkle Watermelon	All Colours	All Colours
Beige	Black True Red Royal Blue Royal Purple Fuchsia	Medium Blue Rose Pink Mauve Soft Burgundy Plum Deep Rose Pastel Pink	All Colours	All Colours
Dark Brown	Light True Grey Magenta Deep Hot Pink True Red White Royal Blue Fuchsia	Periwinkle Orchid Mauve Sky Blue Medium Blue	All Colours	Peach Light Bright Aqua Salmon Orange-Red Bright Golden Yellow
Peach	True Red Deep Hot Pink Burgundy Shocking Pink	Rose Pink Deep Rose Mauve Watermelon	Moss Teal Blue Brown Bronze	All Colours
Rust	Burgundy Blue-Red Fuchsia	Pink Blue-Red	All Colours	Light True Blue Turquoise Aqua Peach

Fashion Colour	Winter	Summer	Autumn	Spring
Mustard	Burgundy True Red Fuchsia	Soft Burgundy Rose	All Colours	Light True Blue Orange-Red
Fuchsia	All Colours	Soft Pink Mauve Blue-Grey	Rust Terracotta	Peach Coral
Grey	All Colours	All Colours	Tomato Red Terracotta Camel Salmon Gold Teal Blue	Peach Clear Salmon Orange-Red Light Warm Aqua Light True Blue Buff
Burgundy	All Colours	All Colours	Rust Terracotta Deep Peach Tomato Red	Light Orange Clear Bright Warm Pink Clear Salmon Coral Pink Orange-Red
Navy	All Colours	All Colours	Tomato Red Terracotta Gold Rust Mahogany	Orange-Red Coral Pink Bright Golden Yellow Bright Yellow-Green
Pink	All Colours	All Colours	Rust Mahogany Salmon Deep Peach	Clear Salmon Bright Coral Clear Bright Red Orange-Red

Many of these fashion colours are neutrals. It is easier to use them with colours from the palettes that allow for co-ordination of the wardrobe and use of proper and complementary makeup. Other colours, including pink, peach, and perhaps some of your favourites, will also work. However, it takes a little more confidence and daring to try the unusual combinations. The results can be really exciting, but only you will know when you are ready to give them a try.

The list of special colour combinations includes all types of each season. With camel, for example, the pine green, true red, royal purple and black will work well for the Winter/Autumn flow individual. The blue-red, burgundy, charcoal grey and fuchsia will work for those who are Winter/Summer and the true red will work for those who are Winter/Spring.

The biggest and most frequently asked question is, 'What about black?' Most women grow up thinking that black is the most basic, most professional and most sophisticated colour that a woman can wear. With the introduction of seasonal analysis, black has become the most controversial of all colours, since it appears only in the Winter palette. Surprisingly, not even all Winters can wear black successfully as a single colour next to their face, as it is the strongest of all colours. But wearing black successfully is now possible for all women who know the rules and limitations, as long as they have the desire and personality to wear it with confidence. Simply be certain that it is worn away from the face or in combination with one of your best colours. Remember that the intensity of your makeup should be heightened if you choose to wear it as a single colour.

Here are the guidelines that will enable you to expand your use of colour.

COLOUR GUIDELINES

Single seasonal palette

It is important to understand the single seasonal palette, learn to appreciate balance and harmony, become adept at recognising and working with your best colours. Identify those colours within the palette that are not your best and understand why.

Seasonal palette and flow colours

Add flow colours to individualise your seasonal colours. It is only by understanding your seasonal flow that you can understand your unique colouring.

Seasonal palette, flow colours and use of fashion colours

Once flow colours are used successfully and comfortably, add fashion colours. Those who prefer a high-fashion look will be eager to begin to wear these colours. Those who are most conservative may decide to work only with flow colours.

Use of all colours

Those who want an extreme look may choose to use all colours, regardless of balance and harmony with their colouring, to make a pre-determined statement.

Colour definitions

You are now ready to create any look you wish, as you now understand the elements of style. You may find these definitions useful:

Dramatic colours are bright, vivid and deep, providing a lot of contrast.

Elegant colours are rich, deep, muted and have little contrast.

Rich colours are deep, intense and strong.

Delicate colours are light, bright and clear.

Vibrant colours are vivid, bright and clear.

Pastel colours are light and soft.

Sharp colours are deep and clear. A sharp line or picture has clarity and contrast.

Matt colours are soft and muted.

Natural colours are deep, rich and earthy.

Classic colours are neutral.

Romantic colours are any that create the mood for your own definition of 'romantic'.

ENDS AND BEGINNINGS

Women who wish to explore more colour choices for themselves are learning ways to wear all colours, how to co-ordinate their new colours with their existing wardrobes and how to create unique looks in order to satisfy their individual needs. You can now have your own personal style – your own line, scale and colours.

Now you understand how your body line and personality may be most effectively expressed by the styles and colours of the clothes you wear, you will know how to be always in style.

INDEX

ORDER FORM

□ **ALWAYS IN STYLE FASHION PORTFOLIO** £14.95 (inc. VAT, postage)

Attractive portfolio folder available twice a year, Autumn/Winter and Spring/Summer, containing:

1. An over-40-page booklet of fashion trends, including information on fabrics, colours and accessories, with original fashion drawings.

2. A full-colour sheet on fabrics and prints for the season.

3. A full-colour sheet on the fashion colours for the season.

4. A sheet of wardrobe silhouette drawings for your body line.

□ More information. Please send me more information about Always In Style.

□ **SEASONAL SWATCH SETS** £15.95 (inc. VAT, postage)

Contains 30 fabric swatches in a handsome canvas wallet, plus make-up guide. Check your season:

My season is: □ WINTER □ SUMMER □ AUTUMN □ SPRING

□ **FLOW COLOURS** £5.50 (inc. VAT, postage)

Contains flow swatches and a 6-window vinyl holder designed to fit your existing wallet holder. Check your flow season:

□ Autumn/Spring   □ Winter/Summer
□ Autumn/Winter   □ Winter/Autumn
□ Autumn/Summer   □ Winter/Spring
□ Spring/Autumn   □ Summer/Winter
□ Spring/Summer   □ Summer/Spring
□ Spring/Winter   □ Summer/Autumn

If you would like the name of a consultant nearest to you, or information on how to become an Image Consultant, call: 01–627 5211 or write to: Always In Style, FREEPOST, London SW8 3BR.

ALWAYS IN STYLE, FREEPOST, LONDON SW8 3BR.

Please send me what I have marked. I enclose my payment (cheque/money order) for _____

NAME (Mr/Mrs/Miss) _____

ADDRESS _____

_____ POSTCODE _____

SIGNATURE _____ For telephone orders: 01–627 5211.

Please allow 14 days for delivery.